Nobody
had heard of
HAY

Nobody
had heard of
HAY

The Hay-on-Wye book that
celebrates the Millennium

LOGASTON PRESS

LOGASTON PRESS

Little Logaston, Logaston, Woonton, Almeley, Herefordshire HR3 6QH

First published by Logaston Press 2002
Copyright © Hay Millennium Society 2002

ISBN 1 873827 12 1

Set in Adobe Garamond by Giles Morgans & Pat Welch and printed in Great Britain by Biddles Ltd

CONTENTS

ACKNOWLEDGEMENTS

The following people have all contributed in one way or another to putting this book together, in alphabetical order, because this is the only fair way. They have given their time freely whilst the costs incurred in publication have been paid by means of a grant from the Millennium Commission coupled with financial and practical assistance from Logaston Press.

Lesley Arrowsmith   who did a magnificent job of editing a mass of dictated or roughly compiled interviews, researched architectural details and also undertook some interviews herself.

Brian Bentley   who took nearly all of the photographs, in particular, the pull-outs, which required days of patient observance.

Anne Brichto   who oversaw the whole thing on behalf of the Millennium Society but let the committee get on with it.

John Field   who interviewed several people, drew up the vital timetable and liaised with Logaston Press.

David Howard   who was the original Chairman, but had to resign due to other pressures but conducted one of the most fascinating interviews before he left.

Betty Maura-Cooper   who took over the Chair from David, learnt how to delegate and conducted lots of interviews, putting them on disc for Lesley to edit.

Dennis Mills   who also had to give up before the book was ready to go to press due to other commitments but helped with his professional input initially.

Giles Morgans & Pat Welch   who sorted out all the really difficult bits - design, type-setting, lay-out, scanning in the photographs, and without whom this book would not have been possible.

Haydn Pugh   who is also a photographer and helped out with all sorts of nitty-gritty stuff.

Karl Showler   who kindly contributed the Appendix and portrait of 19th century Hay and led two of the promotional conducted tours.

Robert Soldat   who wrote the Brief History, without which the book would lack being placed in historical context.

Photographs contributed by Eric Pugh, Vera Fairfax, Mary Davies and Betty Maura-Cooper and, of course, all those people who kindly gave of their time to be interviewed.

PREFACE

This book is about Hay-on-Wye, its buildings and the people who have lived and worked in those buildings. It was decided to concentrate on the 'heart' of Hay, and to that end the 'pull outs' include photographs of buildings in Broad Street, Lion Street, Castle Street, and High Town along with some adjoining areas. Members of the Hay Pages Committee, who compiled this book, interviewed residents of the town and recorded their memories and tales of incidents and events that happened in those streets, interviews which make up most of the book.

The book commences with a brief history of the growth of Hay to the present day - in itself a fascinating tale that ends in the no less fascinating evolvement of the book trade which now ensures that this tiny town is internationally renowned. It has been produced by a small group of volunteers on behalf of the Hay Millennium Society. Everyone involved has worked hard interviewing long-term residents of the town; transcribing these interviews; editing and typing all the words; planning the style, layout and design of the book; taking hundreds of photographs; having them developed, researching and writing the history of the town; liaising with the publisher; attending many committee meetings and even taking conducted tours of the town in order to promote the final outcome of their labours. It has been very much a team effort and the reward will lie in the enjoyment and appreciation of the people who buy this unique book about a unique town, Hay-on-Wye.

Reading the description of Hay as it was in 1934, it is hard to believe that this prosperous, thriving little town was once so poverty stricken. Although its inhabitants today could not, by any manner of means, be described as wealthy, they have the pleasure of living in a busy, lively community. For Hay is not a 'ghost town' with deserted streets and empty houses in which stranded pets are left to their own devices all day whilst their owners commute to distant places. On the contrary, a stranger strolling through the town would witness everyone going about their business, greeting each other by name, with dogs lolling contentedly in doorways, and a tortoiseshell cat dozing on a pile of books. We are lucky in that we still have two family-owned butcher's shops and a greengrocer's, together with two small grocers, which, even though they are owned by large chains, are still staffed by familiar 'locals' and retain their individuality. Then there's the health food shop that has just about everything anyone would need for the most exotic of recipes. There is no supermarket actually in Hay (it's over the border in Herefordshire!) and the town has such a small year-round population that there is no danger of one being imposed.

For people visiting from some other parts of the British Isles, it must be like stepping back into their childhood, yet for all its lack of shopping precincts and the soul-less 'pedestrianisation' with which so many places have been blighted, Hay has not fallen behind the times. It has a superb web-site (www.hay-on-wye.co.uk), with several of the bookshops offering internet book searches and it is, overall, the envy of many other places which are trying to create a similar 'book town'. It has taken 30 or 40 years for Hay to evolve into the internationally famous book town it now is, and which is responsible for its relative prosperity. There is, perhaps, a danger of there being only book or antique shops in the future but hopefully a sufficient number of people will continue to shop in the town for their food, electrical goods, gardening needs, newspapers and clothes for these shops to survive. Hay does not want to become a 'living museum' and there are enough strong characters in the town to prevent this happening.

Talking of strong characters, although this book is about buildings and streets, what has made the stories about them is the people who lived amongst them, and that is what Hay is really about; from the most famous individual to the latest newly-born baby, Hay is a place to celebrate life.

Betty Maura-Cooper, Chair, Hay Pages

A Brief Account of the
First 800 Years of The Hay

THE NORTH VIEW OF HAY CASTLE, IN THE COUNTY OF BRECKNOCK.

HAIA, Y GELLI, or y.̃ HAY, was destroy'd A.D. 1216. by Lewis y.̃ Dauphin of France; who in y.̃ Reign of K. John was Invited into England by y.̃ Barons. It has been y.̃ Poſseſsion of y.̃ Boyles, afterwards of y.̃ Gwynnes, & now belongs to Rich.ᵈ Wellington Gen.ˡ)

Sam.ˡ & Nath.ˡ Buck delin. et Sculp.ᵗ Publish'd according to Act of Parliament Mar.ᶜʰ 25 1741.

A Brief Account of the
First 800 Years of The Hay

POLITICAL HISTORY

Hay, or The Hay, is just over 900 years old. There is no knowledge of anything on the town site before the Normans built the castle sometime around 1100.

The vicinity, however, shows signs of habitation from as long ago as the Stone Age, as the long barrow at Pen-yr-wrlodd bears witness. The Twyn-y-beddau round barrow, the stone circle at the car park below Hay Bluff, standing stones and traces of ancient huts at various places in the mountains show a continuous line of settlement stretching through the Bronze Age and into the Iron Age. Hay itself was the site of two fords, one by the Warren and the other by Newport Street. A bronze axehead, pottery fragments and other finds bear witness to the use of both the fords in those times.

The Romans constructed a large camp at Boatside Farm, just across the river from Hay. This camp may well be the site of a major defeat inflicted on the Romans by the native Silures, which Tacitus reports (c.50AD). However, this was a minor setback for them and the Hay area subsequently spent nearly 400 years as part of the Roman Empire.

After the Romans left (traditionally in 410), part of the present county of Powys became the Kingdom of Brycheiniog, named after Brychan, its founder. He had twenty-four saintly daughters and eleven saintly sons, although there is some dispute about precise numbers. According to legend, there was already a local saint, St Igon, daughter of Caradoc/Caratacus, who founded the church at Llanigon around 60AD, possibly the first church in Wales. When the Church was organised into parishes at the end of the Roman period, that of Llanigon included the land one day to be Hay.

The area passed obscurely through the border wars and raids of the Dark Ages to re-emerge in the record with the coming of the Normans.

They came to the Hereford area early. Edward the Confessor had stayed at the Norman court when he was in exile in his youth and had close family connections with the Norman ruling families. It was on account of this that his cousin Ralph, later called 'the Timid', established an earldom along the Wales-Hereford border, with the help of a group of Normans. Here they built the first stone castles in England (c.1050), at Hereford, Richard's Castle and Ewyas Harold. It has been argued that Mouse Castle, above Hay and just in England, was one of this series or a Saxon copy, but there is no hard and fast evidence either for or against.

In 1055, Gruffydd ap Llewelyn, the only Welshman to rule all Wales, allied with the renegade Saxon Earl Elgar, attacked and defeated the Normans, probably owing to a decision by the Normans to put Saxon foot soldiers on the backs of horses that they could not control in battle. They proceeded to burn and sack Hereford, including the cathedral where the bishop was killed. The next year the new bishop, Leofgar, and the Sheriff of Hereford led an army of reprisal into Wales, which was defeated with much slaughter at Glasbury. A truce finished this little war and it was not until 1063 that the final English response occurred when Harold Godwinson invaded Wales and Gruffydd lost his life.

Harold never colonised Wales as he soon had other matters on his mind but after the Norman Conquest, the new King of England saw Wales as a threat to be conquered or contained. He appointed a series of 'Marcher Lords' to hold the border and when possible advance it into Wales, and gave them almost royal powers. The local man was William fitzOsbern, Earl of Hereford, one of the Conquerer's closest and most trusted advisors. This redoubtable warrior achieved much in the five years before his early death in a feud in Normandy, most notably the building of a string of castles along the border, including one at Clifford. He also gained a notable victory over three Welsh rulers in the area of Hay. This may have been the battle at the foot of Hay Bluff remembered in local folklore when the streams ran red with blood.

William's early death, in 1071, followed five years later by the revolt and dispossession of his son weakened the Norman presence on the border. It was not until the late 1080s that another land hungry baron, Bernard of Neufmarché, began to colonise the Wye Valley through Glasbury to Talgarth. He too revolted against his king, William II, but was taken into the king's peace, provided he did something more useful with his time.

Consequently he built Brecon Castle. This led to an attack by the local native ruler, Bleddyn, backed by his overlord Rhys ap Tudor, which culminated in the battle of Brecon, fought in 1093 near the village of Battle. The Normans defeated and killed them both and created the lordship of Brecon. After that there were no more kings in Wales.

All this is important because Hay was founded by these same Normans, as a base to secure their lordship at the point where it came closest to England. The exact date of Hay's founding is unknown; it could be any time from the late 1080s onwards but our first record of the settlement comes in 1115 when the parish church of St Mary was dedicated. As it was given a church and separated from its mother parish of Llanigon, it must have already achieved a certain level of population. William Revel was tenant under Bernard of Neufmarché, Lord of Brecon and Hay.

Hay Castle was built during these early years, almost certainly an earth and timber structure initially. This first castle is usually identified as the motte opposite the rear entrance to the Swan Hotel. Later, when the focus of the town shifted, the castle was moved to the site of the present stone structure, between Castle Street and Oxford Road. However, another school of thought sees them as simultaneous structures, representing two different manors, one centred on Hay proper, and the other centred around the church and the site of the present cattle market car park. No definite evidence exists to settle this either way, but it is worth noting that the site of the Oxford Road Castle overlooks the site of the cattle market castle; further, having a pair of castles guarding an important centre is far from unknown at this rather unsettled time. (Talgarth boasts seven in its immediate environment and Brecon castle has at least five outliers).

It is also worth noting that the church of Hay, St Mary's, is outside the town boundaries, with a chapel of ease, St John's, in the town. This also suggests two separate parts to the early town of Hay.

From its foundation Hay shared a lord with Brecon; these lords appointed deputies to manage Hay rather than leaving it to a feudal vassal, so the history of Hay has much in common with that of Brecon for most of the following 400 years.

Bernard of Neufmarché had a son, Mahael, who was disinherited. Gerald of Wales tells us that Mahael found his mother, Nest, with a lover, whom he beat severely. She, in revenge, went before the king, Henry I, and made a statement to the effect that her son was not the son of Bernard but of another lover. This self shaming statement, presumably untrue, was believed by the king, who had also enjoyed the lady's favours. Consequently the lands of Brecon passed to Bernard's daughter, not his son. She married Miles of Gloucester, High Constable of England, in 1125, who thus gained her lands.

Miles was a champion of Matilda during her war with Stephen for the crown, but he died prematurely in a hunting accident. He was succeeded in turn by four of his five sons, all of whom died without an heir. The lands were duly divided between their sisters in 1165, the Brecon-Hay portion falling to Bertha, who had married William de Braose of Builth. Within ten years he was dead and the lands passed to his son, also William, and his wife Maude, neé St Valery, otherwise known as Maude Walbee. She was the Lady of Hay, this manor being her particular responsibility and source of income. She has passed into popular tradition as a giantess who built Hay Castle in one day, having gathered the materials in a single night. One of the stones for the castle fell into her shoe; this so annoyed her that she threw that stone all the way to Llowes, where it can still be seen as St Meilog's Cross in the village church.

In fact, she was a formidable character who helped her husband in his empire building in south-east Wales and personally led the force which captured Painscastle. This fortress was subsequently besieged by the Welsh and it was at Hay that the relieving force, under the Justiciar, Geoffrey FitzPeter, mustered prior to their overwhelming victory at the battle of Painscastle in 1198.

Maude is responsible for the first stone castle at the Oxford Road site, parts of which remain to this day.

She and her husband, William, went on to greater things when John became King of England in 1199. They were particular favourites of his and he loaded them with lands and offices of power until almost all south-east Wales and much else besides was in their hands. However, a few years later, in 1207, they suddenly fell from favour. John sought reasons to quarrel with them and turned these disputes into offences against the Crown and thus an excuse to sieze their lands. Some say that this trouble came about because William de Braose had witnessed John kill his nephew, Arthur, in 1203. When, four years later, John annoyed Maude by an unreasonable request for her sons as hostages for good behaviour, she let slip that she knew of the murder and might not keep quiet. After this they had to be silenced. John took their property, including Hay, but the de Braoses withdrew to Castell Dinas and harried the local countryside in what amounted to a small war. Eventually they burned Leominster but were forced to flee by John's foreign mercenaries in 1208, leaving for Ireland only to be followed, a couple of years later, by John. William fled to France, but Maude and her eldest son, also William, were captured and starved to death by John, probably at Corfe Castle. William died the following year, 1211, in France, still a fugitive.

William and Maude had two sons who survived them. These took advantage of the war that sprang up between John and his barons to retrieve the family fortunes. They were Giles de Braose, Bishop of Hereford, an opponent of John even before the family's feud with the king, and Reginald, his warrior brother. With the tacit support of Llewelyn the Great, they rapidly regained many of the family's original holding of castles in Breconshire and southern Radnorshire with the active support of the Welsh rulers of Elfael. This campaign, in 1215, and other troubles in Wales brought John himself to the border, where the following year he burnt Hay, both castle and town, to teach everyone a lesson. Other matters soon took John away to the eastern side of England, and he died in Newark the same year. The death of John and the establishment of a regency for the child king, Henry III, under the popular William Marshall, Earl of Pembroke, led to a gradual process of reconciliation. Reginald de Braose came into the king's peace in 1218, Giles having died in 1216. Hay was rapidly rebuilt and repaired.

At this time, trouble was never far away. The last de Braose lord of Hay, another William, was hanged by Llewelyn for adultery with his wife Joan, King John's illegitimate daughter. Soon after, in 1231, war broke out along the border between Richard Marshall, Earl of Pembroke and Prince Llewelyn on the one hand and the king's forces on the other. Once more Hay was set to the torch, this time by Llewelyn. Later that same year an English force was defeated near Hay, partly through treachery by the monks of Abbey Cwmhir, for which they were subsequently heavily fined. After this things settled down, and in 1234 Hay was given to Eva de Braose, neé Marshall, William's widow, as a dower. This second 'Lady of Hay' seems to have presided over a period of peaceful reconstruction. The town was rebuilt, the castle repaired, a project initiated by Henry Turberville, the custodian from 1233-34, and a murage grant for three years, from 1237, meant proper stone walls could be built around the town itself. Although most of the stone fabric of these walls has disappeared, probably taken for domestic building, the associated banking remains in very many places and allows an accurate plotting of most of their course. Eva de Braose held Hay until 1244 when the de Braose heiresses took possesion of their various portions of the late William's lands.

Hay formed part of the allocation to William and Eva's daughter Eleanor and her husband Humphrey de Bohun, eldest son of Humphrey de Bohun, Earl of Hereford and Essex and High Constable of England. However, Roger Mortimer, who had married Eleanor's sister Matilda and received the lordship of Radnor from the de Braose legacy, considered the Bohun share was too large and claimed Hay and certain other castles for his own share. This dispute rumbled on through various courts and enquiries for years and although Roger Mortimer and his wife and mother received various payments they never obtained any land. By 1263 war, of varying fortunes but generally favourable to the Welsh, raged between Llewelyn ap Gruffydd and the Marcher Lords. Meanwhile a major quarrel was brewing between the king's party, including Prince Edward and Roger Mortimer, and the barons' party, led by Simon de Montfort and supported by Humphrey de Bohun of Brecon amongst others. It is in this context that, after the fall of much of the land of Brecon to the Welsh, Prince Edward transferred Brecon, Huntingdon and Hay Castles to Roger. Brecon was later surrendered to the Welsh, thus Hay, for a time, became the caput of the remnant of the

Lordship. However, a few months later, after his victory over the royal party at Lewes in 1264, Simon de Montfort took the surrender of Hay from Walter Hackelutel, Mortimer's man, and Hay was back with the Bohuns. It was through Hay that de Montfort passed the next year on his way to sign the treaty of Pipton, near Three Cocks, with Llewelyn, when he was recognised as Prince of Wales. Then a few weeks later the barons were defeated at Evesham, Roger Mortimer personally killing Simon de Montfort with a savage blow to the throat. Hay reverted to Mortimer. The next year Gilbert de Clare, Earl of Gloucester and Lord of Glamorgan, the great power broker of the day, took up the cause of the dispossessed barons. Many confiscated lands were restored and Hay returned to the Bohuns. The Bohun claimant, yet another Humphrey, was a minor, his father having died a prisoner at Beeston Castle of the wounds he received at Evesham, so Gilbert de Clare held Hay on his behalf. Another year passed before the then of age Humphrey de Bohun took control of Hay on the payment of a large compensatory payment to Mortimer. Thereafter the Bohuns held on to it for over a hundred years. Hay was the only part of the Lordship of Brecon not then in Welsh hands and thus was the young Humphrey's base as he attempted to reconquer his patrimony, a task he achieved by 1278, in the wake of the general defeat of Llewelyn.

After this, Hay's role in history declines. The final defeat of Llewelyn and the Welsh meant many of the Welsh castles became less and less significant. However, the coming of peace must have led to the flourishing of trade and simple industry in the town of Hay; indeed despite the turbulent careers of her Bohun lords Hay seems to have been left undisturbed. When the last Bohun died he was Earl of Hereford, Essex and Northampton, Lord of Brecon and High Constable of England.

The surviving daughters of such a potentate had to marry princes, as indeed they did. Mary married Henry, Earl of Derby, and Eleanor married Thomas, Duke of Gloucester, both of the blood royal. Hay was part of Henry and Mary's share. Henry later became Henry IV and spent much of his reign at war with Owain Glyndwr and his 'free Welsh' warbands. Rumour, as reported by Leland, suggests Hay was damaged by the Welsh but the official record does not bear this out. The responsibility for Hay's defences were given to the Earl of Arundel with Sir Richard Arundel as constable. Local landowner John Bedell and his son organised local resources in addition to a garrison of sixteen lances and eighty archers, which suggests Hay was able to hold its own. Also, no claims for major damages exist from this time.

Hay Castle continued to be maintained, as did the walls, well into the 15th century, long after the disappearance of Owain Glyndwr. (A status report of 1453 will be noted in the section on the castle building.) Glyndwr himself very likely spent many of his last years at the house of his daughter and son-in-law at nearby Monnington-on-Stradle. He may well have visited Hay, perhaps on the main fair days, quietly, in disguise – an intriguing thought!

After Henry IV's death in 1413 Hay passed to his son Henry V, who took a strong contingent of troops from the Brecon Lordship to his war in France. Most of these were a body of bowmen, a quarter of whom came from Hay, thus Hay archers helped win the battle of Agincourt.

In 1421 Henry, son of Mary Bohun, carried out an exchange and re-division of the great Bohun inheritance with Anne, Countess of Stafford, daughter of Eleanor Bohun; as a result she became the holder of Brecon and Hay Lordship. Her son and heir the Earl of Stafford, was created Duke of

Buckingham in 1441. Hay was by now a small part of a large estate and consequently saw little of the lord himself. His powers were usually wielded by the Steward of Hay, an office which was significant at least from the time that the Bohuns arrived, and still extant today.

Hay was by now in a gentle decline, still busy but not to the point of filling all its potential burgage plots. It also suffered, to some extent, from the general lawlessness which occurred because of the poor rulership of Henry VI and his advisors. The Black Mountains and the Radnorshire hills harboured many people who easily turned to banditry when government control was weak. The period before and during the Wars of the Roses gave free rein to all this for many years. A major factor here was a long running 'war' of raid and counter raid with the men of Elfael. Continual complaints are aired – damage to the town and its walls are mentioned, as well as the holing of the town boat and the theft of all the doves from the lord's dovecote. In 1450 things reached such a pitch that John Scudamore, the Steward, was commissioned to raise sixty men-at-arms-from the manor and thirty from the borough 'for the defence and safe keeping of the town for fourteen days and nights against the enemies from the Lord of Elfael'. Even the Yorkist ascendancy only slowed this down, further complaints occuring in Henry VII's reign. Not until Henry VIII sorted out the lawlessness of the Marches once and for all at the time of the Anglo-Welsh union did this problem go away. This little publicised feud was obviously serious and similar complaints from those in charge at Bronllys and Talgarth in the mid-15th century corroborate that banditry was endemic in Elfael. However, the troubles were blamed for every failing in that time. It is entirely possible that the drinking of building allowances and the 15th-century equivalent of false insurance claims may have played a part here as well.

The three Dukes of Buckingham who ruled Hay all met violent deaths. The first was killed at the Battle of Northampton in 1460; the second was executed for treason and rebellion against Richard III in 1483, and the third was executed for treason by Henry VIII in 1521, although the latter's only real crimes seem to have been his wealth, his pride and his royal blood, all of which made him a potential rival to the king. Hay was taken into Royal hands along with the rest of the duke's lands, although Henry, Lord Stafford, the duke's son, may have held Hay for a while among the land re-granted to him by the Crown. However, it was the Crown, in the person of Henry VIII, who granted the castle and Lordship of Hay to James Boyle in 1545. By another account, it passed to him 'by some irregular means'. This was two years after the official union of England and Wales in 1543. It was then

AT THE HAY
Published by Geo. Wood, London 1814

At the Hay 1814

that Hay ceased to be the second town of a major Marcher lordship on a national border, and became a small country town in one corner of one of Wales' new counties, a long way from the national centres of power and influence.

SOCIAL CONDITIONS

Before continuing the story of Hay it is useful to backtrack a little to see what the ordinary townsfolk may have been doing throughout the Middle Ages. Generally the records for Marcher lordships have seldom survived. However, whenever a lordship was taken into Royal hands, usually when a lord died and the heir was a minor or arguments between a number of co-heirs needed arbitration, an Inquisition Post Mortem was taken, and several of these survive in the better kept Royal records, along with a few other interesting items. These inquisitions provide an inventory of a lord's lands and income, usually with the names and obligations of his tenants.

These tenants, in the town of Hay, were all English or Anglo Norman. The Marcher lordships were generally divided into two, the land over 600ft above sea level, roughly speaking, being the Welshry where the Welsh law ran, and the land below 600ft was the Englishry, where the lord's law ran. The lord's law was based on the law of the March, which in turn was similar to the law of England – similar but not the same for the king's law did not run in the Marches and each lord made his own law in his own estate.

The Englishry of Hay consisted of the town and the lands covered by the present day parish of Hay, together called Hay Anglicanae, and the lower part of Llanigon parish, Thomas Kirke/Llanthomas, the upper part of that large parish being Hay Walensis. Hay, as with many other Marcher towns, was initially limited to English and Anglo-Norman residents. These were lured in by generous terms for free burgesses in what was effectively a dangerous place to live in a war-torn border. Each town was an outpost of the colonising race in a foreign land which could, and did, become hostile at frequent intervals. Each town was usually equipped with castle and walls to protect this relatively privileged colony, the members of which would turn out to help man these walls in time of emergency. Hay followed the usual pattern; the documents concerning the Welshry are full of Welsh names while the town burgesses are exclusively bearers of Anglo-Norman names. Further, the Englishry is divided into borough and manor, the town and the rural areas respectively – each had its own court and its own laws and customs.

The burgesses of Hay paid a fairly easy rate of dues, but had to use the lord's mill, oven and brewery, all of which included charges to the lord in their prices. They had to agree to occupy the minor offices of the town when their turn came, attend at least three courts in a year plus the day of the March court once a year. They also had to do some work on the lord's land or pay for another to do this. They would probably own strips of land for their own support in the same field where the lord had his, as well as their small burgage plots within the walls. They must join in the 'hue and cry' of criminals when called. In return for these duties they enjoyed the protection of the town defences and a near monopoly on local trade, with weekly markets and annual fairs (at May and Michaelmas), when people would come from miles around to trade and enjoy the larger than usual range of goods plus entertainments and side shows. The lord collected dues on all the trade that took place in the markets, which is why 'forestalling' was a crime. This was the practice of selling goods on the way to the market, outside the area of the town and therefore not giving the lord his 'cut'.

A document exists from the middle of this period (1340), giving the extent of the Lordship of Hay. It includes a full statement of a typical tenant's dues and responsibilities:

John Gille holds 2 burgages from the lord for himself and his heirs and owes suit at three lawful hundred courts without summons and shall come to a day of the March for the hundred and Lord's court for three days if he is in the lordship. If fit and in the town he shall come to the hue and cry in the town, if he should hear it, and in the lordship with the Steward or his lieutenant whenever it is commanded or shall be amerced 12d in the Lord's court. If summoned he shall go with the lord or his lieutenant at his own costs within the lordship wherever the lord wishes for one day. If the lord wishes to have him longer or outside the lordship then he shall be at the lord's pledge. He shall be portreeve, catchpole or ale taster if elected. He shall give the lord …. ale from which he brews. He shall do suit to the lord's mill, bake his bread at the lord's oven, help to lead the water of Duueleis when necessary to the said mill [a reference to the water channel carrying some of the waters of the Dulas brook from Cusop along Heol-y-dwr to the mill pond in Broad Street where Underhills petrol pumps are now] and shall pay 2/6 at the Annunciation and Michaelmas yearly.

From translation of *An extent of the Lordship of Hay 1340* by Richard Morgan, *Brycheiniog,* vol. 28

This comes from about the middle of Hay's time as a Marcher lordship and is typical of the whole period, as regards obligations and privileges, although the monetary sums may vary. Twenty-two burgesses are listed, assuming there is no case of two people with the same name, among whom are several Walwyns, a Waldeboef, Dun, Attebroke, Scut, Budell, Baker, three Bonghams and the chaplain of the blessed Mary. Women as well as men held land and paid dues. From the Welshry the lord was owed dues of labour, money and a tribute of pigs; if the tenant had three or more, the third best pig. He was fined one cow or 5/- if he hurt another Welshman. He must attend the 'hue and cry' – the general pursuit of criminals and outlaws. The tenant of Glinhotheney also owed attendance at three courts, and accompanying his lord, or deputy, one day each year. He must also pay 4/- if his daughter married, or if she is 'corrupted'. There were also two military fees in the lordship, Clannogh (Cilonow?) held by Phillip de Clannogh in 1340 (who also held lands in Herefordshire of different lordships including Cusop) and Thomas Churche (Llanthomas, the lower part of Llanigon village including Llanthomas Castle) held by John le Bruet in 1340. Both were held by attendance at court and one military fee, being the provision of one man at arms for castle guard for twenty days at the tenant's cost.

In 1340 Hay seems to have been thriving, the eleven burgage plots shared by the twenty-two burgesses had risen to eighteen and three-quarter burgage plots, the precise number of burgesses unknown, in 1368. Hay's population would have included the burgesses' families and a number of 'borrelfolk' – common people. 1368 perhaps was a high point. Although Hay, along with the rest of the uplands of Brecon and Radnor, escaped the first two visitations of the Black Death, showing it to be off the main English trade routes where the plague raged, a fall in collectable rents suggests the third visitation of the disease, in 1369, took some toll. Thereafter, trouble including the Glyndwr rising and the bandit war with Elfael meant Hay experienced slow but definite decline. The town was unable to attract new settlers in the 15th century and the increase in pastoral, as opposed to arable farming, in the rural areas together with some burgage plots permanently unoccupied speaks of a general fall in population and prosperity. Nevertheless, the bills for repairs of the castle, the walls and even the lord's town ferry boat suggest a place at least being maintained. Hay eventually entered the union with England as a quiet, slightly rundown, but still active and, above all, pleasant place.

THE SHAPE OF HAY

Mediaeval Hay was an enclosure within roughly triangular bounds. Outside were the river, then crossed by boat or ford with the Dulas brook flowing out of nearby Cusop, and the water channel down Heol-y-dwr, along with the castle's meadows and orchard, the church of St Mary's and associated buildings. Separating all these from the town were the walls, eventually made of stone, and the castle. The walls were punctuated by three gates close to the corners of the three-sided town, in addition to which there was a small postern gate. More will be said of these later.

Early Hay sloped away from the gateway and keep of the castle and had two principle streets. One took in Belmont Road, Broad Street, and Newport Street; the other followed roughly the line of Castle Street and then probably bent round the castle to run down Bear Street. A large area running downhill from Castle Lane, including the Bull Ring, Market Street and High Town, as far as St John's Chapel, served as a market place. The market place had taken its present shape at least by 1740.

A further street ran down Heol-y-dwr, connecting the other two streets, and may likewise have fronted houses with burgage plots. Just what happened in the spaces in the middle part of the town is unclear, although it seems there was much open ground, if the 1684 engraving of the Duke of Beaufort's artist, Dineley, reflects the earlier state of affairs. A number of other Welsh walled towns had similar open spaces, for example Chepstow.

A major point of interest about Hay is that, although hardly any buildings survive from before 1543, the plan of mediaeval Hay is still easily seen on the ground. In many parts of town the houses have been built on the same burgage plots since Hay was laid out. The house shapes and long thin burgage plot gardens survive, for example on the north side of Broad Street and in Bear Street. The old street plan together with the connecting street and lane has not changed significantly over the years. This together with the 'old world' style of many of the Hay houses means a very strong feel of mediaeval Hay can be obtained in some parts of the town. As John Leland wrote in his *Itinerary*:

When I approchid nere the Hay and began to discend from thens, I saw on the hither side of Wy a good mile from the Hay the Castle of Clircho. After passing over Wy River, the which for lak of Knowleg yn me of the Fourde did sore troble my Horse I cam in crepusculo to the Hay. The Hay standith hard upon Wy and yt shewith the Token of a right strong Waulle having in Hit iii Gates and a Posterne. Ther is also a Castel the which sumtime hath bene right stately.

Within the Toune is but one poore Paroche. In the Suburbe hard by Wy is a Paroche Churche meately fair. There is also in the Suburbe a Chapel wher on a Sunday I hard Messe. Not far from the Paroche chirch in the Suburbe is a great rounde Hille of Yerth cast up by Mennes Hondes other for a Wynd Mille to stond apon, or rather for sum Fortres of Bataille.

The Town of the Hay yet hath a Market but the Toun within the Walles is wonderfully decaied. The Ruine is ascribed to Oene Glindour.

One shewid me in the Toun the Ruines of a Gentilmans Place called Waulwine be whose meanes Prince Lleuelin was sodenli taken at Buelth Castel and ther beheddid and hes Hedde sent to the King.

Dulesse a pretty River rising in the Montinnes about iii Myles from the Hay cummeth even through the Toun and strait into Wy without the East Gate of the Toun. In Feldes hard by a Ploughyng hath be founde oftimes numismata Romanorum, the wich ther comminly be caulled Jewis Mony.

The Toune longgid to the Duke of Bockingham. It pertaineth now to the Lord Staford his Sonne.

The Mediaeval Defences of Hay — Wall & Castles

Hay was a completely defended town for its first 500 years. As mentioned, one castle site is found in the corner of the cattle market car park behind the Swan. It is a broad mound with a flat top suggesting this held a wooden ring work; a tower or stonework usually leaves tell-tale lumps of rubble even after the best stone has been used elsewhere. There was apparantly also a bailey but any trace is now hidden under the car park.

The town walls were probably an earth rampart above a ditch with a palisade above for the first 100-150 years. It is not until 1237, after at least two burnings, that a murage grant is recorded for full stone walls. These were probably built six foot thick, buttressing the old bank and rising above it. The line of these walls is fairly well known and easily perceptible in many places, as the land has either been scarped or banked, giving an obvious change of level between the interior and exterior of the ramparts. There are almost certainly buried footings at certain places, the stretch between Bear Street and Oxford Road being a good example. The line of walls to the back gardens overlooking the Dulas brook to the east of the town probably includes some original stonework.

If approached from England Hay would have been entered from the Newport Gate, which was situated close by where Newport Street and Wyford Road meet beside the old Lamb Inn, now a vet's. The line of the wall ran south from here and is easily discernable where it overlooks the Dulas brook meadows. The wall probably followed the inside of the lane beside the Black Lion, swinging round to Black Lion Gate, which straddled the road adjacent to the eponymous pub. The wall line between here and the castle is represented by the change in level, easy to see, between the back gardens of Oxford Road and those of Bear Street. The wall then either ran behind the castle, between it and the current market place, so separating the castle from the town, or simply ran up to the castle wall, joined it and took off again on the other side, thus incorporating the castle in the defences of the town. Considerations of economy and spatial relations incline the author to the latter argument. From the castle the wall ran along the embankment separating the levels of two back gardens behind the Blue Boar, crossed the street at Carls Gate and followed, probably, the wall of the cattle market down the lane to the river. The Carls Gate plaque and small niche to mark its site have probably been shifted a little for the gate was more likely situated just west of the Castle Street/Cattlemarket Lane junction. The final stretch of wall ran along the river bank and turned beside Wyeford Road back to Newport Gate. The railway cutting has removed all trace of the walls along the river.

The walls have declined quietly over the years, doubtless helping provide building materials for many a Hay house. The gates were all demolished sometime in the latter half of the 18th century. It should be noted that no-one knows the location of the postern gate, probably just a small pedestrian entry, however hints in an old bill for repairs to the wall, and the current ground plan, suggest either the Oxford Terrace/Oxford Road junction or the Backfold/Oxford Road junction.

Hay Castle is the oldest building in the town. Although with all its rebuildings it is difficult to say just which parts are truly ancient and just how old. Paul Remfry has advanced the intriguing idea that the tower goes back to 1070 and represents one of William fitzOsbern's chain of early castles. If this were so it would make it contemporary with Chepstow keep and thus joint first stone castle in Wales. The architecture of the keep could fit in with this but it has been rebuilt and rebutressed so many times that it is impossible to be sure.

Whether Hay Castle followed the motte near the church or was contemporary with it, there is little doubt that it predated the legendary building by Maude Walbee. It was probably a single earthwork and wooden palisade in its early days except for the tower which, very likely, was the first structure of any kind on the site. Maude de Braose was probably responsible for rebuilding the walls in stone, after the famous visit there of Gerald of Wales and Archbishop Baldwin, when they met the people of Hay on the castle steps when preaching in support of the Crusades. The two burnings of 1216 and 1231 doubtless damaged the castle but there is nothing to suggest it was destroyed; the inner part of the gate and the surviving section of wall, although much repaired, almost certainly represent the work of the 'Lady of Hay'. The castle stayed essentially the same throughout the Middle Ages, periodically falling into decay, periodically being repaired. Its last repair as a castle was work ordered by the 3rd Duke of Buckingham. As a staff including Constable and Porter were kept on until the castle was sold to James Boyle it was presumably still in use even if run down. The Boyles used it as a residence, so habitable apartments remained; but around 1650 these were replaced by the mansion still visible today. About this time most of the walls were demolished to improve the view from the new house. Early prints show that, from the late 1600s, the silhouette of the castle has changed very little. Today, as when it was built, it still dramatically dominates the town.

The keep tower, although essentially very early, has been much repaired and rebuilt, possibly because of poor foundations. The north and south walls, (the front and back), have both been rebuilt and the windows reset in new places. The tower has also been butressed at every corner at various times. It had a roof and battlements; the battlements fell early, but the roof appears not to have been removed until the 19th century.

A rumour suggests this was done, and the hole knocked in the upper storey, to make a 'romantick ruin'. The tower has three stories over a partial basement and walls five feet thick, quite thin walls by the standards of the day.

The tower may have had an entrance from the side where the mansion now stands, but it retains its entrance on the other side at first floor level. This is reached by a stair, which turns right by the door and follows the line of the top of the gate arch to reach the wall walk. The gateway itself is a fine Norman arch, but a later structure surrounds it. Some time after the original gateway was built a 'jerry-built' gatehouse was added. This put extra arches both within and without and created a chamber above the gate with a slot to accommodate a portcullis. The carelessness of the build is illustrated by the outer arch on the town side which is obviously unbalanced, a result of bad planning, not collapse; unsurprisingly this has now had to be braced. It is entirely possible that the door now in place under the arch dates from the mediaeval heyday of the castle.

A section of wall runs away eastwards from the gate. It appears to be full height except for the battlements. The place where it breaks off suddenly gives an interesting cross section of a mediaeval wall, with a carefully laid 'skin' on both sides and a rubble infill; the whole is about six feet wide. At the time of writing this feature is obscured by ivy. The battered plinth may be original but could equally be later buttressing. Most of the rest of the wall is traceable by virtue of mounding and even some outcrops of masonry. The wall curved all the way round to where the mansion house now stands, but the present entrance from Oxford Road was probably formed when the mansion house was built, for it breaches the old wall line.

The mansion is a fine Jacobean building dating from the mid-17th century, a particular glory being its brick chimney stacks. These bricks were brought into the area from elsewhere and their cost of manufacture and transport led them to be seen as status symbols when used as profusely as in these structures. The ground floor level, now a bookshop, shows many interesting old features, which could relate to the castle's high status building, which probably stood on the same spot. The upper floors have some antique interest but this is limited by the ravages of two fires, one in 1939, from which time the tower and east end of the mansion have remained gutted. The western end of the building was restored after this only to suffer a further fire in 1978 which has required further restoration. The castle currently belongs to Richard Booth, self-styled King of Hay, the originator of Hay's status as a second-hand book capital and thus the creator of the town's present prosperity. 'Good King Richard' has spent generously on the restoration and preservation of the building, but this kind of old structure can prove a black hole for finance.

Finally, what did the old castle look like in its time of greatest use? The view of the castle from the north bears strong similarities to the way it has always looked. The gateway steps originally went right down to the street level in a straight line. The area these steps traversed, roughly the green banks between castle wall and today's perimeter wall, were a kind of outer bailey but probably not defended, merely kept clear for the field of fire and given over to cultivation and grazing in quiet times. It is probable that the high status chambers of the castle and its banqueting hall would have been where the present mansion is. It is the best site in the whole enclosure, requiring defence only on the northern side which faces into the town anyway. The south facing front of these buildings looks into the body of the fortress and is thus safe for large windows and other features which favour comfort over defence. These buildings would probably have been lower in height than the present mansion.

The tower, even when roofed, was only a few feet higher. The gatehouse and wall are almost as they always were. The missing features can be guessed at with some hope of accuracy, partly from archaeological observation, partly from written records, particularly an account rendered in 1453 by the then bailiff, Phillip ap Gruffydd Lloid. The mound that roughly surrounds the present day garden almost certainly represents the old wall line. This is borne out by outcrops of masonry at points on the east and south sides of the enclosure. The fact that the 1453 account speaks of the tower in the singular, quite definitely referring to the tower still extant, suggests that there were no other towers or turrets. This in turn suggests a classic ringwork castle: a plain wall running in a huge curve away from the main buildings, encircling a large court, and then returning back to the main buildings. In this type of castle all the buildings would have been built penthouse fashion against the inside of the wall. The inner court would have been open space. The rise in ground level just inside the mediaeval gate suggests that the original court now lies four to six feet below the present surface. Beyond this little can be said save to list a few features mentioned in 1453 but no longer extant. These include a bridge requiring a lock and at least partly made of wood. This may have been a drawbridge outside the main gate, but precise information is lacking. The castle also had a barn divided into a stable and a haystore and a well. A great chamber and solar, a lord's private room, also existed, mentioned separately from the tower and thus probably not in it, perhaps part of the high status buildings where the mansion now stands.

THE LATER HISTORY OF THE HAY — 1543-1876

Although at the Union of England and Wales Hay finally ceased to have much national significance, it still retained a relative prosperity as a local centre of trade, a place where local food stuffs and materials could be exchanged for the goods, especially manufactured stuffs, of the outside world.

There are many strands to the story of Hay's journey from the middle ages to modern times. One strand is the later story of the castle. The Boyles and their successors the Gwynns did not have a happy relationship with the town, both being accused of tyrannical behaviour. James Boyle was fined by the Government for illegal collection of tolls while his bailiff was accused of beating up stall holders, two of whom claimed in their wills to be dying of injuries thus sustained. James' granddaughter Mary married Howell Gwynn of Trecastle. They succeeded to the property around the turn of the 17th century and commenced building the mansion at the castle soon after. They continued in the high handed and unpopular manner of Boyle and worse, and numerous complaints were received by the Court of the Star Chamber against them, some by no lesser figure than Eustace Witney, a former sheriff of Radnorshire. To extortion and violence they seem to have added a case of illegal imprisonment, and in addition also tried to cheat the Crown out of ownership of Welsh Hay. They were subsequently fined and excluded from Welsh Hay, but confirmed in ownership of English Hay where they seemed to have carried on as before. Howell was followed by his son Thomas who in turn was followed by the joint tenure of his two children Howell and Elizabeth.

Hay, wisely, seems to have played no part in the Civil War It was visited by the Duke of Beaufort on his vice-regal procession through Wales, when he was royally entertained at the castle. It is to his artist companion Dineley that we owe some of the earliest pictures of Hay. Frances Gwynn, who died in 1702, in her will endowed the Gwynn almshouses, first by the Dulas Brook and now in St Mary's Road. After this the castle was let as apartments.

One of the tenants of the castle during this period deserves special mention; the French born imposter George Psalmanazar. He had come to this country after an adventurous early life, including a Jesuit education which left him fluent in Latin, a time as a soldier and then as a wandering adventurer. During this time he would represent himself as an Oriental to gain sympathy, interest and support. He later settled on a 'Formosan' identity and invented a language, culture and religion to go with this. Few people having travelled to the Far East, he was able to get away with this especially as he clearly possessed a fine intellect, ready wit and a good dollop of genuine learning. He published a *Description of Formosa* complete with bogus autobiography in 1704 and was received with warmth at the highest levels of society. He impressed the (Protestant) English by abusing the Jesuits. He later fell on harder times as people refused to be impressed, however he always found some support and earned some money by writing on genuine scholarly topics such as Hebrew and History. After a serious illness in 1728 he renounced his former life and devoted himself to scholarship, Dr Johnson regarding him as one of his best drinking companions. It was only a year after his death in 1763, that his 'Memoirs' were published and in which he confessed all. When he lived at Hay is unclear.

Later in the 18th century the castle was sold to Richard Wellington. He was followed by Henry, another Richard, and another Henry. During this time the lordship of the manor was held by the Harley family, of whom the Earl of Oxford was head. It is through this link that the Harley family endowed the Harley Almshouses and how Oxford Road gets its name. This road also contains Oxford House, once owned by the eponymous Earl. It is rumoured that the first Earl to own the house bought it from the family of a girl called Rosanna who lived there and of whom the nobleman was deeply enamoured, but unfortunately the lady did not return his love.

Around 1800 the castle was leased out, first to Joseph Bailey of the Nant-y-glo steel dynasty and later, around 1826, to Rev Williams Allen, the first of three clergymen in a row to occupy the place. Meanwhile Joseph Bailey bought the lordship of the manor from the Earl of Oxford in 1833 and the castle from Henry Wellington in 1844. However, he continued to let the castle on a lease. The Rev Williams Allen, a mostly absentee vicar, was followed by the Rev Walter Wilkins (1830-35 at least). By 1840 Rev Humphrey Allen was in residence. He had been stipendiary curate of Hay – the man on the spot who actually did the work – since 1831 and was instrumental in getting the old church of St Mary's pulled down and replaced with the present building. It is due to the rebuilding that the only truly old features of the church are the tower and some tombstones and effigies. It is impossible to say if this was a great architectural loss, but it certainly created a lighter, more practical building and swept away the 'owned pews' which had come to take up three-quarters of the church and were hardly ever used. Thus everyone could now worship at a seat and in comfort. Allen was independently wealthy and met a considerable amount of the cost out of his own pocket. He also contributed to the founding of the gas company and over a quarter of the total cost of the National School. He was both a hard worker and a great philanthropist and was much missed when he moved to Holy Trinity in Bristol.

The next occupant of the castle, in 1845, was the Rev William Latham Bevan, the first resident vicar in Hay for over a hundred years. He lived there for more than fifty years and was a classically cultured, vigorous, philanthropic clergyman who did much to improve the quality of life in Hay over and above his pastoral duties. He became utterly attached to the town, refusing four chances of promotion because they meant moving away. Like others before and since, living in the castle made him feel like a king and his autocratic manner is remarked upon. However, he worked tirelessly to improve the lot of those less fortunate than himself, was helpful to the needy and a strong advocate of temperance. His greatest contribution was in the field of education, doubtless on the principle that if people had learning they had the potential to conquer all other problems. He caused the National School in Hay 'to put its act together', arranged for workhouse children to be admitted and improved standards. Two years after he started this campaign the school was commended as one of the best in Wales and with the highest percentage of children in the community attending of anywhere in the country. He always emphasised that teaching the young to read and to love books would improve them and help to keep them from the ale house; promoting books is nothing new in Hay! He also created the Hay Literary Institution out of the moribund Hay Mechanics Institute. The Working Men's Club was revived and the British School formed with his help. A scholar himself, he contributed to several ecclesiastical publications. He also gave the Parish Hall, Lion Street, and the Infants' School to the parish, paid for from his own pocket. He held open house to the society of his day and the Rev Francis Kilvert, curate of Clyro, was a frequent visitor to him and his wife and four daughters. When he finally left Hay in 1901 he was sorely missed.

The castle was briefly home to the Rev Smith, the next vicar, then to Col. A.E. Morell, but on the death of Lord Glanusk, head of the Bailey family who owned it, in 1906, it became the home of his widow the Dowager Lady Glanusk and her daughters, still remembered for good deeds to those in need. 1937 saw the castle sold to the rich banker Benjamin Guinness MP, whose only achievement seems to have been to let it burn down. It fell to the next owner, Mr V.E. Tuson of Clifford Castle, to restore it. Eventually the castle came to be the property of Richard Booth.

Hay's progress through Tudor and Jacobean times seems to have been quiet and uneventful. The Acts of Union (1536 and 1543) had brought Wales under direct Crown rule and law uniformly applied across the country. Further the rigorous application of that law by the Lord President of the Council for Wales and the Marches, Bishop Roland Lee – he is said to have hanged 5,000 people – put an end to casual brigandage and local wars. Hay was uninvolved in the Civil War, that conflict's only obvious effect being the arbitrary dismissal of the local priest, Thomas Dennis, by the Parliamentary appointed committees who oversaw the clergy. There was no replacement for ten years.

Hay was, like many small rural towns, partially cut off from the outside world, though in Hay's case the isolation was compounded because the local roads were in an appalling state. These 'roads' were largely dirt tracks with little solid composition, a factor which became troublesomely obvious whenever it rained, a not uncommon occurance on the Welsh border! The result of little repair and constant erosion was huge ruts and numerous pot-holes, problems which the local parish-by-parish repair gangs, recruited from the locals as a form of parish dues but for limited time periods each year, were entirely unable to keep up with. Wheeled traffic was only possible (most years) in good weather in summer and the favoured form of carriage locally was a horse or ox drawn sledge until well into the 18th century. Pack horses made up some of this deficiency, but even they could not travel in the worst weather. Barges came up and down the Wye, but they could not get to or from Hay if the water was too low or if the river was in spate, thus they could hardly be relied on. This poor system of communication meant that while Hay never became 'industrial' in the true sense of the word, it was a hive of small industry because the majority of the needs of life had to be obtained locally.

Records for the town of Hay are 'thin on the ground' until the mid to late 18th century so it is only possible to surmise prior to that. However, Geoffrey Fairs gives the following trades and industries and there is every reason to believe things had not changed much over the preceding 200 or more years. In Hay, around 1770, the trades of saddler, perukemaker (wigs), tailor, carpenter, blacksmith, mercer, flaxdresser, watchmaker, brazier, carrier, cooper, and shoemaker all existed. To this list can most likely be add those of miller, baker, nailmaker, all kinds of builder, (plumber, stone layer etc.) tallow chandler – candles were more or less the only form of lighting – butcher, and grocer. Only a few innkeepers are evidenced but as Hay later had numerous public houses, it may simply be a case of under recording. Tanning, fulling and flannel-making are all noted in later years. There was even a brief outburst of barge-building which produced at least two barges during the early decades of the 19th century. The more anti-social trades, anti-social by means of smell, noise or similar disturbance, tended to be found clustered near the Water Gate in Newport Street. Here the prevailing wind and fall in the land protected the more salubrious parts of town from the worst of the negative aspects of these industries. Further abundant water, drawn from the Hoel-y-dwr channel or from the Dulas and the Wye, helped power and cleanse the various little industries. A mill, a tannery and later the Gas Works were all found down here.

The community Hay was serving with all these necessities and conveniences was, of course, the rural society. It was their products which Hay could trade to the outside world. 'The commodities are cotton, corn, cattle, fish and some otter' wrote Dineley in 1684, cotton in those days being a preparation of wool. Earlier, in 1631, Hay was referred to as 'the chief cornmarket of the County' in State papers, while ever since the Black Death thinned out the rural population sheep farming, carried out to produce wool with meat as a by-product, had flourished in the area. Later the best Hereford Cattle were found in the Hay hinterland. The Wye was, until recently, a fine fishing river with plenteous stocks and apparently the only river in Britain to carry all the native riparean species.

Although gentry, farmers and tradesmen tended to do well there was always a section of the population who found life less prosperous. There were numerous people including whole families who fell into poverty. Throughout the 16th and 17th centuries there was constant expenditure on relief of the poor, some of whom lived at home and others in lodging houses which received regular payments from the Vestry, the assembly which performed local council functions. These paupers were expected to do useful work in return for the financial help, if any such work could be found. Later, in 1837, the workhouse regularised this system, where its size bears testimony to the scale of the problem. It still exists, nearly complete but recently converted into flats behind houses, in the area bounded by Brecon Road, St Mary's Road and Gypsy Castle Road.

The Welsh parishes were already diverging from English practice with a greater emphasis on 'out relief' – the payment of a small sum to people who continued to live at home, rather than the English system whereby the paupers were brought together in great workhouses, segregated by sex and age and given tasks to perform in house.

Even if not a pauper the lot of the local labourers was often not all that good. However, if wages were low beer and cider were cheap. Hay possessed a large number of public houses – 34 at one stage – in a town whose population never rose above

2,000, a significant proportion of whom were of the temperance persuasion. It has been said that in Hay you were either temperance or a drunk, there was no in-between and sayings tend to contain a germ of truth. Another extravagent statement about the town which is perhaps truer in spirit than in actuality, is that Hay was a sea of mud and drink with a bit of fornication thrown in. Given the number of pubs and an illegitimate birth rate which peaked at 46.5% in 1847, two of the above propositions have at least a grain of truth. As to the mud, there was no denying that Hay could be a very dirty place and given the amount of rain in Wales, the town must have been bathed in a rather unpleasant mud fairly often. The mud would have included excretia of the horses used in transport and that from the various animals in the livestock markets held in the streets, as well as from the dogs and pigs which ran wild around the place. In addition human dung and rubbish was just piled in the street; one of the local doctors was prosecuted for such a dungheap outside the old vicarage, previously the George Inn in Church Street.

Such prosecutions were the job of the Vestry committee, then after 1865 the Local Board, which consisted of nine elected representatives with salaried officers: Clerk, Medical Officer of Health, Inspector of Nuisances and Rate Collector. These oversaw the running of the town and the gathering of rates to finance this.

This Board oversaw the creation of a piped water supply with a reservoir on Hay Common, which replaced reliance on the seven public wells and various private well. These wells were all outside the old wall at:

Newport Street, the Old Town Well
Black Lion Green, Black Lion Well

The Oxford Road face of the Castle Wall, St John's Well
Beside the west wall of the churchyard, St Mary's Well
Down the path beside the church, the Eye Well
Further down the same path by the river, the Walk Well
Beside the footpath alongside the Login brook, opposite the back of the Swan Hotel, the Swan Well.

However, the sewer system was left unchanged, beyond discharging into the Login and Dulas brooks, the former being extended in 1904 to take the outflow into the Wye. The town rubbish collector was instructed to throw rubbish and ashes into the river. Some improvements occurred over the years but it was not until 1971 that a modern sewerage system was instituted. The Water Company was taken over by the town in 1896, soon after the Urban District Council superceded the Local Board in 1894. Over the years other services arrived in Hay: gas in 1840, electricity in 1913, a modern postal system in 1840, although Hay had been a 'Post town' from before the times when such things were recorded, and a fire service before 1843.

With regard to those two pillars of welfare, health and education, it may be said the 19th century saw a great improvement. The first recorded reference to a doctor in Hay is 1737. Sporadic references during the next ninety years suggest some medical presence, but it is only from 1825 that there are regularly doctors in the town. As for education, a variety of schools existed from at least the mid-17th century but only really devloped with the reforms encouraged by the Rev Bevan in the late 1840s. These put primary education on a firm and successful footing. Although some forms of secondary education were occasionally available in Hay, it has usually been necessary to travel elsewhere for secondary and tertiary education.

Religion in Hay pretty much followed the national pattern, lack of funds and absentee vicars leading to a decline in Anglican fortunes during the late 17th and the 18th centuries. This caused the people to turn to 'chapel' – non-conformist sects which flourished in the 18th century. The buildings of six chapels survive to this day and others have disappeared; the denominations included Baptist, Calvinistic Methodist, Wesleyan Methodist, Primitive Methodist and Quakers. These all flourished in the 19th century as did the Anglican Church after Allen and then Bevan breathed new life into it. This strong religious community led to the formation of a number of temperance societies and friendly societies, these latter not necessarily temperance and meeting in pubs. As for the less religious, they carried on as they always had, by drinking more than was wise.

THE HAY IN THE 19TH CENTURY – KARL SHOWLER

The history of The Hay in the 19th century is dominated by three men and, no doubt, their wives: Henry Wellington (1780-1868) who was deemed locally 'a kind of king in Hay', the Rev Humphrey Allen (1800-18?) and William L. Bevan, (1820-1908).

From the middle of the 18th century The Hay, as it was known locally, grew from a roadside village on the route eastwards out of central Wales into a small but prosperous market town. However, by the middle of the 19th century depressed agricultural prices and the collapse of the woollen industry brought the town into a prolonged decline. As time passed much property fell into disrepair, although on the positive side there was a constant addition to the public buildings.

In 1771 the population of the town was estimated at 838; then followed an increase census by census, until it peaked in 1861 at 1,997 inhabitants. Then followed a century of decline so that by 1921 the population had fallen by a quarter, this at a time when the South Wales industrial towns were experiencing remarkable growth.

The prolonged wars with France culminating in those with Napoleon, coupled with steady industrialisation in England and South Wales led to a very considerable demand for meat, butter, cheese and woollen cloth and grain. By the end of the 18th century large and prosperous farms dotted the middle Wye valley and in The Hay a major house building programme commenced. Major, that is, as compared with what went before and what followed. After 1750 large stone three and four storey houses were built in the central area between the castle and the river as well as cottage rows in Chancery Lane and Newport Street. My own house deeds show how in Newport Street one house was pulled down during 1815 and five cottages built in its place on ground running down to 'The waste by the Wye'. These deeds also show that before 1787 the Hay Mill at the eastern end of Broad Street had been rebuilt. Photographs taken just before it was taken down show it was one of the larger buildings in the town. It was connected to a water supply by way of a leet that ran up Heol-y-dwr then along the crest of the deep Dulas valley until it intersected the brook flowing eastwards from Pontybaker. At this junction were two dams that diverted the brook water either northwards to The Hay, or southwards until it ran into the Dulas brook that itself powered both corn and paper mills. Remains of the leet can be found along the edge of the valley together with the two dams.

Next to the Hay Mill, which was involved in the final preparation of local cloth, was a tannery also dependant on water from the leet. Throughout the 18th century finished Welsh woollens were exported to all parts of the British Empire including India and North America.

A large woollen weaving establishment also existed between Castle Street and Belmont Road and may well have been associated with the weavers' cottages at the western end of Castle Street. However, by the middle of the 19th century the main building was converted to a printing works owned by G. Horden and then H.R. Grant.

THE IRON ROAD ARRIVES

In the 18th century without access to a canal or navigable river The Hay was increasingly isolated. Attempts to make the Wye a navigable waterway from Hereford, a small thriving inland port, to The Hay failed due to the unpredictable nature of the river. It was therefore a revolutionary decision to make a 3'6" gauge tramroad from the Brecon and Abergavenny Canal terminal at Brecon eastwards to The Hay, and then to a junction with another tramway at Eardisley and so to the Radnorshire limestone deposits needed in iron smelting and in agriculture and building. By the values of the day these lines represented a major capital investment that included cutting a tunnel between the Usk and the Wye valleys.

The Regency investors in The Hay Railway, as the tramway was called, could not have known that within a generation, after the wars with France were over, the tariffs protecting mainland produce would be repealed. Wheat and cattle prices would steadily decline as supplies flowed in from Ireland and then the USA and South America.

The horse powered railway was completed to The Hay in 1816 so establishing a connection to the Welsh coalfields. The arrival of this first 'iron road' although primitive when compared with the steam hauled railways, made for a fundamental change in building design. The great open wood burning hearths were replaced by coal fires. The old wide flues were adapted for coal burning – the narrow flue and the chimney pot arrived.

Like our railways today the Hay Railway Company owned the line charging a toll to contractors who owned the waggons and the horses of which over 600 were needed. Operation was simple, the waggon trains ran eastwards one day and westwards the next with numerous sidings to serve individual farms and communities. There was no official passenger service.

HENRY WELLINGTON, 'A KIND OF KING IN HAY'

During the Napolenic War there was much concern amongst the wealthy of trouble caused by labourers. Around Hay there was a concentration of such men working on the railway. The then resident in Hay Castle, Henry Wellington, decided that his dungeon, then used as the local lock up, should be replaced by a custom-built gaol at what is now St John's Chapel. The 'St John's' lock up was to last until 1875 when a court house and gaol was built in Heol-y-dwr.

BRITISH BUGS V. NATIONAL LIONS

Throughout the 19th century Hay was a centre for local education with various 'Academies' for those who could afford to pay for an education for their children. The 1818 national survey conducted by Parliament's Brougham Committee on Education reported that 138 children were in various schools in Hay. These were run on a denominational basis. As early as 1813 Edward Goff endowed a school for non-conformists which was, in time, located at the existing school room adjoining the Bell Bank Baptist Chapel, thereafter a new school, 'The British School', was built in 1877 next to the new Court House in Heol-y-dwr. This school has since been demolished although the Court House survives as private houses.

In the years preceding Victoria's accession the Church of England was establishing a system of education called National Schools. One of these schools was opened in Hay in 1827 in the building now used by 'The Loyal Hay' Masonic Lodge in Brecon Road. This school absorbed the 17th-century Penoyre School and its endowment, cost £527 to build and provided for 300 children, but due to the need for children to work, attendance would have been far lower until primary education became compulsory after 1872.

In the 19th century there was a close link between education and religion, most churches offering some kind of instruction to children and well as giving adults a sound if sometimes gloomy knowledge of the Bible. As the town's population grew,   non-Anglican denominations opened or rebuilt their churches. The Baptists at Bell Bank rebuilt their chapel in 1878. The Welsh Presbyterians opened a church in the new road subsequently called Belmont in 1828 and rebuilt it in 1873 at a cost of £700. The Congregationalists opened the large Ebenezer Chapel on an elevated site opposite the Hay Mill with a school under it.   The Methodists had a chapel opened in 1769 at the junction of St Mary's and Brecon roads, but ninety years later after theological disagreements, the Primitive Methodists built a brick chapel down the Oxford Road in 1865, and four years later the Wesleyans opened a fashionably Italianate church with school rooms near to the Oxford road drive to the castle.

The Rev Humphrey Allen must have known The Hay well for his father lived at Glasbury. In 1833, two years after taking up the Hay appointment, he paid a substantial portion of the cost of a total rebuilding of St Mary's Church, leaving only the original tower. This gave the town a fine late Regency church with nave clear of all impediments, a well sited pulpit and a gallery along the north and west sides so that all could see and hear the preacher. Within a generation it was found that the space around the altar was too cramped so a semi-circular extention was built and the altar moved back into this apse. It was then possible to provide choir stalls and a vestry.

Although some provision for the destitute had been made at Gwynn's Almshouse, built on the 'waste' at the mouth of the Dulas brook as early as 1699, by the middle of the 19th century the house was uninhabitable and a set of replacement cottages was built in St Mary's Road in 1878. In 1832, Mrs Harley opened almshouses for destitute women in Church Street and endowed a second block in Brecon Road four years later. In 1835 the Town Hall was rebuilt by the lord of the manor ,Joseph Bailey.

Humphrey Allen, taking advantage of the regular supply of coal coming up the tramway from the canal, organised a gasworks company that built a 'gashouse' on land he owned adjoining the line beside Gwynn's Almshouse behind Chain Alley in Newport Street. The following year the first gas lamps were set up in the streets with flaring fishtail burners. Some time after this the church was lit too.

To complete a most creative 14 years in the parish Humphrey Allen paid off the remaining deficit of £164 on the building of the National School.

THE PRICE OF PROGRESS
Throughout the first half of the 19th century there was a steady increase in the Welsh rural population so that land which had never been cultivated before was taken in hand, and pastures extended onto higher and higher ground. The failure of the harvest in 1838 caused considerable distress. The local magistrates with their parish constables had difficulty in

controlling a growing population and no doubt there was increasing disorder in the town.

At a time when religious sentiment ran high there was a major protest following the establishment of the Roman Catholic bishoprics in England and Wales. At the western end of Broad Street, where the town clock is today, on Guy Fawkes Day (5th November) 1850, the effigies of the Pope and Wiseman – the recently appointed English Cardinal – were burned. The Catholics did not have a church building until 1968 when they purchased the Welsh Presbyterian Chapel in Belmont Road.

The county magistrates established a local police force in 1840 appointing a superintendant and four constables in The Hay based at the St John's gaol. They were in due course compelled by the County Borough Police Act of 1856 to organise police forces in Brecknock and Radnorshire. These forces were in turn united with the Montgomery force to form the Mid-Wales Constabulary.

Generally the police had a no more than averagely difficult time, Hay being not particularly criminal, but very prone to drunkenness and fighting. However, on two occasions at least, things got out of hand, once when the police superintendent was booed and stoned and had to be smuggled out of town and secondly in 1861. In this year it was believed the tolls on the bridge would be abolished, but when the hopes proved wrong a local crowd went wild, broke down the toll gates, threw them in the river and besieged the toll house for two days. It was at least three days before order, and the bridge tolls, were restored.

William Latham Bevan, MA (Oxon) came to The Hay in 1845. Well connected, his uncle by marriage was Joseph Bailey, patron of the living. William Bevan had been educated at Rugby School so it must be assumed he was familiar with the vices of the young men of his generation. Bevan was to prove a widely read man of considerable ability.

Twenty-five year old William Bevan was quick to get involved in the National School, Brecon Road; he also submitted evidence to the Enquiry into the State of Education in Wales, published in 1848. Hay School was praised as one of the best in Wales. His other great crusade was against drink and it is clear that he did not endear himself to the many owners of ale and cider houses in the town.

Within ten years of Bevan's appointment further military upheavals, norably the Crimean War with Russia (1854–56), the Indian Mutiny and the American Civil War, created a demand for agricultural products and raised prosperity in the area.

Bosworth's Clerical Directory, 1887, shows that Bevan held a number of offices at diocesan level including examining chaplain to the Bishop of St David's. His parish is shown as 'St John's, Hay' which had an 'official' income of £200pa. and a population of 2,154; from this it is clear Bevan had considerable private means that enabled him to travel and run a large household. *Crockford's Directory* shows how clergy incomes linked to agricultural values declined at the end of the century; his net income was £161 for 1890 and £157 for 1897.

William Bevan was the author of several books including ones on ancient and also modern geography and the Hereford Mappa Mundi, together with a very readable parish magazine.

WATER FROM THE HILLS RATHER THAN DEATH FROM THE WELLS

It was in 1861 that the population of the town reached its peak of 1,997 inhabitants. There was, however, a negative side to this as about 34% of babies under five years died each year. With this increased population using cess pits and night soil buckets, both the private and public wells in the town must have been very polluted. At the instigation of Henry Allen of Oakfield reservoirs were built on Hay common and water piped to the town in 1863 by a private company. For many years this worked well but as time passed it became more and more inefficient with serious interruptions of supply due to damaged pipes. An additional source was tapped in 1887 but even so, with poor supplies continuing, the Urban District Council decided to purchase and improve the undertaking in 1896.

THE IRON HORSE ARRIVES

The 1860s were a time of excitement in The Hay. A railway was proposed from Brecon to Hereford via The Hay, which would replace the very uncertain coaches, carriers' carts, and pack horses that worked between Hereford and Brecon.

Construction commenced from Hereford with the line reaching Eardisley in June 1863 and Hay in July 1864. The old town walls along the river had to be removed to permit construction westward. It was also necessary to take down the Quaker meeting house built in 1833 by the bridge as it, too, was in the way. Thereafter the Quakers met at Llydyadyway Farm, Cusop.

In 1866 one of the leading banks, Overend and Gurney closed their doors precipitating a financial crisis that sucked in the Hay and Brecon Railway. After various lawsuits and changes of ownership the line was taken over by the Midland Railway Company.

The early trains would have consisted of four-wheel carriages for passengers, 10 ton trucks for coal and goods, and many lime-washed cattle trucks. The Hay exported, as well as animals, a range of rural products such as wood, tan bark and wool which was now sent in bulk to distant mills to be worked into cloth by machine.

The line up the Golden Valley did not reach The Hay until twenty-five years later and then it only managed a very limited service.The coming of the railway would have brought the price of coal down sharply and also opened the way to modernisation in the form of steam driven stationary engines that would power many of the old processes. Even housewives in their kitchens could now cook on coal ranges.

THE WORLD CONNECTION: THE ELECTRIC TELEGRAPH

The arrival of the telegraph was as revolutionary a change in people's thinking as email is today. The telegram carried from the local office by boys on bicycles made the then unimaginable possible. Kilvert the diarist records how people waited for the Archbishop of Canterbury to telegraph the text of the prayers to be said when the Prince of Wales was critically ill. Not only could people communicate with London but eventually to India and America. Through its Telegraph Office The Hay was in contact with the civilised world.

FRANCIS KILVERT DIARIST (1840 – 1879)

Historians of The Hay are lucky as the Rev Venable's curate at Clyro, Francis Kilvert, kept a diary between 1870 and 1879, much of it focused on the area. From the diaries it is seen that life in The Hay was far from dull although for the poor it could be hard.

CHANGE HATS: EXIT THE VESTRY, ENTER THE LOCAL BOARD, 1865

That long established gathering of local worthies – the Vestry – which had striven to cope with an increasingly urbanised town was replaced by a nine member Local Board elected by male householders.

Although the town had a manual fire engine since 1843 the Vestry only provided a fire station by 1858 in High Town.

The new Board with its Medical Officer of Health, Inspector of Nuisances and Rate Collector had increased powers that covered sanitation and housing. From its start the Board faced a major problem in the grossly overcrowded churchyard. People were no longer prepared, when new graves were made, to see their ancestors' remains cast into a common pit. A large new cemetery was therefore established off the Brecon Road, and opened in 1870 by the visiting Bishop of Hong Kong.

A year later another very controversial matter surfaced with the need to establish a definitive list of street names.

No doubt the Local Board was involved in discussions on the building of a public hall and corn exchange but the steering committee ended up by deciding to build the Clock Tower at the end of Broad Street in 1884.

As the close of the century drew near the wind of change started to blow hard in local government – that ancient body, the Justices of the Peace meeting in County Quarter Session, was shorn of its administrative functions which were transferred in 1888 to an elected County Council. This body started to implement improvements in the main road system including the Brecon Road, Belmont Road and Broad Street, Oxford Road and Heol-y-dwr.

ANOTHER CHANGE OF HATS: LOCAL BOARD TO URBAN DISTRICT COUNCIL 1894

As the century ended the Local Board members changed their hats and together with their Clerk put on those of an Urban District Council. Naturally this was still an all male body elected by an all male electorate. Just as their fathers had fretted about the fire engine so did the UDC. In 1901 they purchased a horse drawn steam pump fire engine to be kept in a custom built station at Bell Bank.

The new century was duly celebrated as was the end of the war in South Africa. Queen Victoria died and the town went into mourning; Edward VII came to the throne with rejoicing at his coronation after a nasty appendicitis operation.

In 1908 William Latham Bevan, the man who had so influenced The Hay during the previous half century, died and was buried with his wife under a Celtic cross in the cemetery opened 38 years before.

King Edward's passing was mourned with purple drapes in the church. George V acceded to the throne on 6 May 1910 so entering a reign that takes us well into living memory.

For all its dense population there was in Hay a large amount of open ground that continued to be built over although the demand was not great as the population continued to decline.

The introduction of a weekly pension (25p) for all people over 70 paid through the Post Office from 1 January 1909 was a radical departure which, coupled with the National Health Insurance (NHI) Act of 1911, started to reduce the pauperisation of the poorest members of society. There was an interplay between the NHI and the Friendly Societies who had added social stability by their contributory insurance schemes, which met the more provident workers' costs for sickness and a respectable funeral. These societies, of which there were several in The Hay added colour to the town with their decorative parades. The Rechabite Friendly Society and the Salvation Army continued William Bevan's work to reduce the excessive consumption of strong drink.

The attitudes of the 19th century can be said to end with the First World War where the death and injury of a generation of young educated officers was particularly high. Cusop and The Hay paid a particularly high price, the War Memorial in The Hay showing there was an abnormally high mortality of the future leadership of the two communities:of the thirty men killed, fifteen were officers. The Memorial does not record those who survived but with debilitating injury. The Second World War loss was six officers and NCOs killed and eight other ranks.

EPILOGUE

As we celebrate the end of one millennium and the opening of another, the inhabitants and visitors to The Hay can see around them fragments of modern history. The bridge over the Dulas that carried the tram line; the great Midland Railway goods shed in the Farmers' Co-Operative yard; the Swan-at-Hay where the stage coaches called, and the Drill Hall, once the centre of social and military 'Volunteer' life.

Henry Wellington, Humphrey Allen and William Bevan who dominated the history of the century have left us the bell and bars at St John's, a fine church at St Mary's and that centre of public life the Parish Room.

And, finally, it was William Bevan's daughters who in 1930 purchased and preserved the St John's building in such a way that it now serves both as a centre of public worship and a compact public room complementing their father's far larger Parish Hall.

THE INTERVIEWS

THE INTERVIEWS

The majority of the quotations are drawn from interviews with the many residents of Hay. We have gathered them together in what we hope is an organised manner in relation to the streets where these people enjoyed their lives in Hay-on-Wye.

SOME BACKGROUND COMMENTS AND THE MAY FAIR

This is an extract from the diary of a young man who visited Hay in November, 1934, found by **Vera Fairfax:**

The neighbourhood is sparsely populated; Hay, so far from being a cheerful market town of the kind one meets in Worcestershire and, for that matter in Herefordshire also, is very poor. The streets are all narrow and the shops old and dingy. Behind the shopping streets, such as they are, are filthy hovels, unfit for human habitation. The people who walk the streets appear, many of them, to be desperately poor, and the reverse of robust.

It is new to me to see such slum dwellings in rural surroundings such as these but visits to the neighbouring towns of Brecon and Talgarth show them to be every bit as bad and convince me that conditions are the same all over South Wales. I would like to have one peep at Merthyr Tydfil but at present I can only imagine it to be an enlarged version of Talgarth. We have, on the other hand, walked and driven over remote country roads, barely passable for one car, crossing the mountains. Occasionally

The May Fair

one passes a lonely farm and perhaps a man or a woman riding a Welsh pony from the mountains to the nearest village for the week's groceries. These farmers are the only inhabitants of the wide range of hills.

Such is the land amongst which we find ourselves. The gentry, of whom one sees hardly a trace and certainly not in the shops of Hay, are all very rich and 'county' judging by their houses, many of which stand empty, perhaps like the ruined farmsteads that abound everywhere, never to be lived in again. During this month in Hay there has been one day with a clear atmosphere to give us an idea of the wonderful views we may expect in the summer and we did not fail to take advantage of this heaven sent opportunity.

This extract was published in *The Wye?* magazine and helps to set the scene behind many of the interviews.

THE MAY FAIRS

As so many people had such vivid memories of the May Fair, which extended throughout the town, we have recorded these stories separately ….

…the May Fair easily extended once or twice right down into Broad Street, by the Town Clock [from Kilvert's]. **Rex Jones**

[The May Fairs] used to be on the road in Oxford Road and would extend mainly from just below the Vicarage right the whole length of Oxford Road to where the National Westminster Bank is. Then the ponies and donkeys used to run up and down Oxford Road. They'd continue in the May Fair from Castle Street past the Baptist Chapel and reach as far as where the new estate agent's by the Kilvert's is. There was a boxing show and different things in front of the Kilvert's and I remember there were galloping horses up on the top opposite the entrance to the Cae Mawr field and there was often horses at the War Memorial and the Town Clock. The horses at Oxford Road were Mr Stud's, of course. He married a Hay girl and a terrific amount of their fair came around here. Mrs Stud was a Miss Evans of Cusop. They were Swansea people, the fair people, and had been showmen for generations. Their two children were educated in this area, the daughter at the convent school at Brecon and the son at Christ College. **Reg Lewis**

I saw quite a few of the boxing matches. It was a fellow called Jack Gage used to run them. He was a travelling showman and mainly you could get an exhibition bout with someone out of the crowd or you have a bout with one of the showmen and someone else. If this fellow stuck so many rounds he'd get paid, if he didn't he lost. The thing was, if it was an exhibition bout it was usually fairly close. The showman didn't take advantage of the fellow he was boxing but of course if he stuck six rounds the fellow got £20 or £10 which was a lot of money.

I remember one fellow from Talgarth, they used to call him the Fighting Parson, and he did an exhibition in Builth with this fellow, a nigger called Neil Evans – a very nice chap and in those days they called them niggers – it didn't mean anything racial. Didn't think anything about it and I expect they called us different names! I knew some of the coloured boys who came then. I'd seen them for two or three years and they used to call us Taffys and had different names for the English and the Scots and all that. It didn't mean a thing. But they fought this exhibition in Builth and then when they came to Hay the Talgarth boys wanted money on it. They were betting against the showman that his fellow wouldn't beat their's, see. Well, of course this coloured boy really had to go to town and the fight only lasted a matter of seconds until the Talgarth boy was knocked out, but couldn't understand why.
Reg Lewis

Dick Elkington remembers fighting Frankie Muddiman, another local boy, in one of the boxing bouts during the fair when he was about 14.

My brother put me up to that and I only lasted a couple of rounds. The coloured man who used to come to the fairs was Cuthbert Taylor from Merthyr Tydfil. **Dick Elkington**

There was another family used to come to Hay a lot for fairs - the Sutton family. They were well known in this area, and were Gloucester people. I remember they used to come in November and were always in this area on Remembrance Sunday, which was Armistice Day. They used to come to the service as some of their boys had been killed during the war.

Another thing with the fairs in those days, the Stud family used to try and make sure that they were always here for a Sunday. Now the fair didn't operate on a Sunday but whether it was the horses they had, they had a thing called the Dragons at one time, they were made in the shape of a dragon, like a big coach and you could get seven or eight people in each. The whole of the afternoon on a Sunday, from about 2 till 5, they would run their machine and not take any money. It would be given to the local nursing association, which operated in those days, of course there was no National Health Service, and nurses were kept going by the sort of area, but they donated all the money they took on a Sunday.
Reg Lewis

Mary Davies' father used to do shoe repairs for the fair people and she and her sister had free rides. **Lily Pitt** remembers she spent her money riding on the big horses that came with the fair.

The May Fair was the main event of the year, on 17th/18th May. It was the hiring fair, and had the travelling funfair, which still comes to Hay. There were roundabouts set up at the Clock Tower and in High Town, and hiring went on near the Clock Tower.

There were always an enormous number of people in the town. The lads used to stand around the street corners, hoping to be hired for work. The fair used to go from early in the morning till late at night from the Bullring to the Blue Boar. There were roundabouts and dodgems, sweet stalls and by the Vicarage [George House] there were swings. Where the War Memorial is there were Peter's horses, a carousel with penetrating accompanying music, but nobody seemed to mind the noise. It was always about the 17th May, which coincided with the day when you expected the last frost of the year – you never put out your kidney beans until after the May Fair! **Tony Pugh**

First of all was that we lived opposite the Williams's, Billy Williams, and he had a lot of girls. When I say a lot of girls I mean the three eldest girls, because their Maddy was a younger girl altogether and came into another age group. But Margery Williams, the eldest, was Carnival Queen in – I wouldn't like to say when it was - but she went as Carnival Queen, and they had the fire engine. Billy Williams was also a fireman and of course living opposite I could see from the house out of the window and Margery came out and I really thought that she was a fairy queen because she was the most beautiful girl. She was done up like a bride and they had the fire engine outside with, I think, four horses, steamed up to go and all the firemen there with their brass helmets and Edgar Evans and Billy Williams in their silver helmets. It was all magnificent and I thought it was really wonderful as a small child... One other thing about carnivals that stuck in my memory – Tom Pugh, fishmonger as they were then, and Billy Pugh who had the sweet shop where Number Two is on the Pavement, they had an elephant. I don't know what's become of it now – it can't be in the loft; it must be somewhere in the garage. I don't remember the reason for having an elephant but there was some reason for it. Magnificent elephant. Probably somebody else'll say it wasn't an elephant at all! **Roger Golesworthy**

BROAD STREET

The 1835 *Pigot & Co Directory* provides some of the earliest information about shop premises in the town. Unfortunately, street numbers hadn't been invented, so only the name of the owner and the street are recorded. In 1835, Broad Street was known as Wye Bridge Street, and the following people lived or traded here:

William Higgins, attorney
Thomas Lewis, attorney and clerk to the magistrates
William Pugh, attorney
Spencer and James, attorneys
John Sheen, carpenter, joiner and builder
Benjamin Trusted, coal and lime merchant
    and flannel manufacturer
Thomas Bromage, corn factor
Unit Watkins, currier and leather seller
Stephen Evans, grocer and dealer in sundries

*John Williams, grocer and linen and
    woollen draper
William Acton, maltster (this could have been at
    West House, which is known to be a malthouse
    later in the century)
Maria Brice, milliner and dressmaker
William Smith, nail maker
Thomas Davies, painter, plumber and glazier
    (possibly only one of these professions)
John Millward, stone mason and builder
James Pritchard, stone mason
Nicholas Hathaway, surgeon (at Tinto House?
    Known to have been a doctor's house later)
Henry Proctor, surgeon
Stephen and Walter Williams, tanners
William Powell, wheelwright*

There was also a pub called the Old White Lion, whose landlord was William Pitt. It was only known to be a pub between 1830-40.

    On Thursday, 7 March 1878, members of the Hay Local Board met to

consider the advisability of providing a proper Sheep and Cattle Market and also erecting a Corn Exchange and Public Room.

A scribe wrote of the occasion:

It is sincerely to be hoped that the meeting will 'see its way clear' to carry out these projects, for the present holding of the sheep and cattle markets in the public

thoroughfares is an unmitigated nuisance which we are sure every resident in the town would be glad to see abolished; whilst the erection of a Public Room, centrally situated, would be a great boon to the town, and its use as a Corn Exchange would, we hope, bring about a revival of the Corn Trade which at one time was carried on so actively but which has almost entirely died out for the want of a suitable mart. So it came to pass that an influential meeting discussed the conversion of the old Coal Yard into a place for holding markets and the erection of a building to serve the double purpose of a Corn Exchange and Assembly Room on a site already acquired in Broad Street.

A large attendance of farmers

showed the interest taken in the matter throughout the neighbourhood and it was hoped that both subjects would be achieved in course of time.

The cattle market was later built, though not the Corn Exchange and Assembly Room, and the local council wanted to bulldoze the castle motte to provide more room. Fortunately, they were prevented from doing this, and it still exists at the edge of the cattle market car park.

Monthly cattle markets were held in Broad Street until 1919, when the present cattle market was built. Sheep were also sold in Broad Street. The live meat market was held the fortnight before Christmas, starting at 6.30am, with dealers coming from South Wales and the Midlands. Cafés and pubs were open all day, though the sale itself was almost over by 8.30am. The dead meat market was held about a week later, starting before 4am and finishing by 8.30am.

Apart from the May Fair, it was just a sleepy little market town. Everyone got an adequate living but relied on the farming community to come in on a Thursday. The train played a vital part – it would be fairly quiet until the train arrived at ten o'clock – you used to hear the hum of people coming up the hill just after it arrived. It came from Hereford and picked up people from Whitney, Eardisley, Kinnersley – all those small places along the way. There were

Policemen under the clock tower during the filming of 'Dandelion Dead'

vans from South Wales that came with eggs, chickens, ducks, rabbits, to sell. They'd open their vans and I think they all had their regular customers. They'd be in Broad Street, up from the horse trough to the Granary. I remember going with my father to the Poultry Fair on the Thursday before Christmas when the wagons came in with the poultry. There were paraffin lamps on the corners of the wagons, because we used to go very early in the morning while it was still dark, about 5 o'clock. Discussions would go on and some of the people would refuse to sell at the prices they were offered and would take away their poultry to Brecon or Builth Wells. Then they wouldn't come and buy at our shops of course, and I can remember there was some distress in the shops if they'd had a bad day. We relied a lot on Thursdays.... **Tony Pugh**

On market days there were stalls all along Broad Street and the farmers' wives would sit on the pavement and sell eggs and other produce. **Eleri Golesworthy**

During the May and November fairs the farmers used to come to town to hire the lads for 12 months. People used to open up sweet shops, fish shops etc. during the fairs as there were no planning regulations or anything like that then – you could open up a shop in your kitchen if you wanted. **Mona Morgan**

[On Market day] it was very busy – the traders used to come in about 6.00 in the morning and they were lined up in Broad Street from the bottom almost to the clock and then underneath the town clock there were stalls and different things. I know this might sound a bit stupid but I always remember one old gent used to come there selling patent medicine and his favourite shout was 'this medicine will cure the rheumatic pains in the back, wind in the bowels, stiff joints and broken legs'. I don't know what it was. They used to shout quite a lot, and then the traders down near to the shop were people with eggs and butter and chickens and things like that. They used to buy them in and a lot of them were from the Valleys – Pontypridd and that way – and the farmers used to bring their stuff in and sell it in the streets. Their vans were parked on the left-hand side of the street, so the traffic could get through. I can remember some sale days, sheep being sold on the cobbles opposite. There were three cottages on the cobbles, next to what was the old Tanners Arms. I remember sheep being in hurdles there being sold and my father telling me about the cattle being sold by the clock and the sheep being sold there regularly but I can only just remember the sheep. But that was on a Monday they used to sell and then on Thursdays there were sheep sales at the end of the year, which were the Ram sales and Ewe sales as they were called. They were held in fields like the playing field that's now on Brecon Road, and the fields behind the cattle market. The farmers' wives used to bring in butter and eggs and some of them used to sell their own, others used to sell it to the traders mostly from the Valley areas. They used to bring in live chickens and ducks, especially towards Christmas time. I know when we lived in Broad Street you could hear them coming about 5.00 in the morning. It was a dark time of the year and they'd be in before it was light. I remember one old farmer bringing his own in and he was well known for his meanness. He'd come to Hay, then he took them to Talgarth, then to Builth and in the end he had to bury the lot because he couldn't get the price he'd asked for! **Reg Lewis**

I used to get 6d to drive the cattle from the cattle market down to the station and lead them up on the trucks. I can't remember how they used to clean up the streets after! **Dick Elkington**

CLOCK TOWER

The clock tower was built in 1884 by J.C. Haddon of Hereford. It originated in a legacy by Captain Brown for a clock for the church tower. The idea was expanded by the executors to include town clock, public hall and corn exchange but only the tower was built, at a cost of £600.

Hay was a more rural place then. On Boxing Day there was always a hunt with thirty or forty riders but nowadays there are only about fifteen.
Eleri Golesworthy

Broad Street during the filming of 'Dandelion Dead'

There were celebrations round the town clock on VE Day, with street parties and everyone had a great time. **Mona Morgan**

When I was being born, Doctor said to Mother, 'I've just been to see Mrs Armstrong.' So that was going on while I was being born and subsequently Mother says there were police up in the clock tower watching Mr Armstrong going to have his pint because the pub was not open on a Sunday, but they used to work a private client arrangement. His place of tipple on a Sunday morning was the King's Head, which was opposite us, now called Tredegar House. I don't know what they were doing up the tower but Mother says they were. **Roger Golesworthy**

The Council offices were the Vicarage. Eric Pugh's shop in the Pavement was the Labour Exchange (now electrical goods). The photographic shop [on the Pavement] was a barbers; they used to call him Sweeney Todd, or Sniff & Blow, because he used to sniff then blow the hair away from your neck. **Dick Elkington**

The telephone exchange was underneath Nino's [now the Booksearch Café] and our bedroom window was just over the road. We used to be able to hear what they were saying on the phone and heard all the gossip! My father-in-law said his father had taken him to see the dancing bear and the bear was kept behind the railings at the end of Nino's by the telephone exchange and he felt very sorry for the bear. This was at about the turn of the century. **Eleri Golesworthy**

They had drawn the tar barrels down Belmont Road with wire ropes after a wonderful display of fireworks. The dying embers lay round the Clock. Broad Street was deserted. It was 2 o'clock and a bitterly cold November morning. From my bedroom I espied two figures in each other's arms. They broke into song – 'Rescue the perishing, care for the dying'. Dick Chip and Harry Rosser. I took them down some whiskey and told them to get along home. They floated into the night. The landlord of the King's Head was T. Wright. **Wisps of Hay**

My father lived in Hay and he told me that as a boy he used to work at the King's Head [now Doll's House 2] and in the mornings he had to take a broom and sweep the swill out through the door! There was a lot of drunkenness in those days. Another time he was in the Band of Hope church parade coming down to cross the road by the Loggin Cottage where there was a stream across the road. They were singing away and his pal pulled his sleeve and drew his attention to his pal's Dad who was lying half in and half out of the stream, dead drunk. They just left him there to sober up! **Tony Pugh**

> Little drops of whiskey
> Little drops of gin
> Lead from paths of virtue
> To ruin and to sin
>
> Little drops of Allsops
> Little drops of Bass
> Take away the senses
> Make a man an ass
> Little drops of brandy
> Little drops of rum
> Take the cash from many
> And the lives of some
>
> But little drops of water
> Will never disagree
> And water pure and sparkling
> Will be the drink for me

Victorian poem contributed by Vera Fairfax

…the Overseers on January 22nd, 1781, decreed 'that the house adjoining The King's Head be rented by Us from Mr Joseph Tanner for the use of Elizabeth Price and family, that is supported Weekly at the expence of Hay and Llanigon, and to pay YEARLY, the rent or SUM of Thirty-six shillings. **Wisps of Hay**

A Mrs Stapleton made cakes and sold them from her shop next door to the current Country Casuals. She had a fire in 1926 and moved down the road to where Edgar Evans lives now. **Mac Maddy**

The Bridge in 1935

UNDERHILLS GARAGE

There used to be a brook that ran from Oxford Road into Heol-y-dwr, right opposite where the Police Station is now. It was an open brook right down to where Brook Street runs into it, then under the road again, and then it used to come out below where Underhills Yard is now. There used to be a millpond where the forecourt is now. The brook ran into it and there was an escape down into the river. It's been diverted into the Dulas brook now. **Rex Jones**

Where Underhills garage is there used to be the mill pond, a big square. There was a wall round it because there used to be a brook ran down Heol-y-dwr and I fell in the millpond trying to get a ball. I fell in the mud and they had to get me out with some ropes. **Emma Dunn**

The garage where Mr Underhill is now was a man called Spencer Hall, who retired and went to live in Weston and lived till about 90.

Talking about poaching, as youngsters, there were three or four of us, only about 14 or 15 and we used to lay night lines down the river. Coming from the river one night we were coming past the Lamb, a public house that's now the vet's at the bottom of Ship Pitch, we were coming round there and a certain old gent from Hay was lying prostrate on the floor there and we struggled to get him up. We got him up into the top of Ship Pitch and at the old Mill in Hay where

Mr Underhill's garage is now, there was a Mr Randall who was a very religious old man and a very nice old boy. When he saw this fellow, drunk, he said, 'Well, I can't refuse to help but I don't like to see people like that. Bring him in the Mill'. We took him in and laid him down on some sacks, searched his pockets on Mr Randall's instructions and found some matches, which we took off him, and covered him over and left him for the night. In the morning, I came out into Broad Street and there was the old boy looking a bit shaky. I said to him, 'Hello, how are you this morning?' 'I'm all right,' he said. 'Why shouldn't I be?' and I said: 'You were drunk last night'. 'I wasn't drunk, boy,' he said, 'there were two men holding me down'. **Reg Lewis**

Where Jane Underhill is used to be a garage. They had a great big garage where you drove in. **Emma Dunn**

PINOCCHIO'S

The Pizza Parlour was a saddler's and he did shoemaking a bit as well, but mainly repaired harnesses and made saddles and collars for horses. **Reg Lewis**

Where Pinocchio's is used to be a leather shop. He used to be a tanner. He made saddles, bags, everything – those legging things. **Emma Dunn**

ROGUES GALLERY

I worked there as a schoolboy after school and on Saturdays when Frank Webb kept a cycle shop in Broad Street. I was serving petrol mainly and repairing bicycles. The main things that he was selling were bicycles and accessories and they had two petrol pumps there, one which was in the alleyway between the two shops and one which was out on the pavement, quite close to a gas standard that was in the street there. It's next door to the Pizza Parlour. There were two old sheds at the bottom and another small shed in the yard. On Thursdays, when the market traders used to come, they had their vans and lorries at the other end of the street and they used to store their stuff in the shed at the bottom. They had been stables at some time as the mangers were still in there. I went there when I was three and they weren't being used as stables then. **Reg Lewis**

Next to that used to belong to Webbs [the undertakers] where Rogues Gallery is. They used to serve petrol there, and they used to service radios there – the accumulators for radios. Lallies had it as a bike shop next because I bought a bike from there.
Emma Dunn

3 BROAD STREET, THE OLD HOUSE

I didn't work in Broad Street for very long but I lived in Broad Street at No 3, which is next door to the Three Tuns. **Reg Lewis**

Humphrey Webb's daughter Julie still lives there. **Emma Dunn**

The Three Tuns and the Old Bridge

THE THREE TUNS

This is the oldest secular building apart from the castle in Hay, according to Geoffrey Fairs. The Three Tuns and 3 Broad Street were originally a single building, comprising a hall and solar wing. The present structure dates from around 1600, though probably on earlier foundations. In 1835 the landlord was James Byran, who was also a dyer. In 1891, Edward Lloyd was the landlord. In the 1920s, the landlord was Mr Powell, father of the present landlady, Lucy Powell.

Then there was Mr Powell at the Three Tuns. Lucy, his daughter, is still there today. **Reg Lewis**

Of course, the Three Tuns is still there, and people tell me that lady is the richest lady in Hay. I saw her tonight walking back from the Co-op and you'd think, well, with her amount of money she'd at least get a taxi, but no. There was a guy used to get in there, a bit of a tearaway actually. She had a dog in there and it was a bit of a pest sometimes, he'd lay down on the floor and kick his feet up in the air. Well, you know, he was in a bad mood and he got hold of the dog saying 'I'll give it bloody dog!' and carted it down to the bridge and chucked it in the river, off the bridge. When he came back he said, 'Now we'll have a bit of bloody peace'. Three or four minutes later, in comes the dog back through the door. If she'd known what had happened to it she'd have gone spare. **Charlie Evans**

Lucy's was always a pub. Her parents had it. **Emma Dunn**

THE BLACK SWAN

It was known to have a licence from 1684. In 1835 James Pritchard was the landlord, in 1891 Mrs Mary Ann Powell was the landlady and in 1926 Thomas Price was the landlord. It was delicenced as a pub in 1946, due to illegal betting on the premises, and is now a private house. The building is probably of 17th-century origin.

And then the next one up, the Black Swan, there were lots of people there, you know the landlords changed every few years. The first one I remember was Mr Price and it went on through until in the end when I joined the RAF at the start of the war, there was a Mr Bound there, who was a Londoner who came with the evacuees and he'd taken over. I don't remember much then as I moved away. **Reg Lewis**

Lily Pitt remembers that the evacuees didn't like it here – they said they got their milk in bottles!

The Black Swan used to be used a lot during the war because they always had a piano going in there. Very popular. I went down there without my mother knowing. **Emma Dunn**

A few years later, we moved to the Old Black Swan, No 5 Broad Street, where, 47 years later, we still live.

When we had been living there about a month, we were sitting chatting by the fire one night when in the room above came such an unholy noise, just like someone tipping a load of wood. The children began screaming and spent the rest of the night all in one bedroom. On inspection upstairs, everything was quiet again and in spite of a thorough search indoors and out, nothing was out of place. Possibly 'Fred' had found us again, I thought. [See 15 Castle Street] About two weeks later the row began again, but still nothing was found, since then all has been peaceful, although my granddaughter insists that this house is haunted and won't venture anywhere in the house alone. I am quite sure that whatever it was that happened that night, if it was evil, it was on its way out and decided that we were more than welcome to stay here which we have and it is a beautiful old house and certainly nothing 'spooky' is here now.

As a postcript I will just say that in 1937 I bravely stepped inside the front door of the Old Black Swan and had a half pint of shandy – women didn't frequent public houses much in those days – little knowing that I would spend so many happy years here.

Incidentally, it isn't a public house now, the license was taken away sometime during World War Two owing to illegal betting going on. **Amy Price**

REST FOR THE TYRED

The date on the front of the building is 1623 but the style of building is earlier – it's almost certainly an old burgage plot, with a long narrow site and garden behind. It has been the Café Royal Restaurant and Bar, Colin's Restaurant and Fisher's Bookshop and is now the Broad Street Antique and Book Centre, with Rest for the Tyred B&B above.

Rest for the Tyred in Broad Street was Hitchcock's grocers with a café behind it, that Mrs Hitchcock used to run. **Eleri Golesworthy**

The other main grocers was Hitchcocks, who ran the Wye Hotel (now the Penny Bun) and had a bakery in Broad Street. **Mac Maddy**

The next two shops were owned by Mrs Hitchcock who was grandmother to Mr Gittins who's got the Garage at the bottom of our street here [near the Black Lion]. **Reg Lewis**

Next door was his mother's shop which was a bakery, sold bread and cakes. As a kid I've been in there for a pennyworth of broken biscuits and Eric Hitchcock said to me, 'Many times I was glad of the penny. **Emma Dunn**

Miss Hitchcock was a maid at one of the big houses in the area, and became concerned that the young master of the house was interested in her. Not wishing to become pregnant and lose her job and her character, she looked around for a way to become independent. She approached one of the solicitors on Broad Street and asked him to loan her the money to buy the shop. He was so surprised by her audacity that he did, and she opened a grocer's shop. **Mary Fellowes**

No. 7 Fish and Chip Shop
The building is dated 1896 on front, and initialled TW, possibly a member of the Wellington family of Hay Castle. It has been the Post Office.

Hitchcock's shop was where Dai Ratcliffe's got his fish shop. **Emma Dunn**

No. 8 The Butchers

The butchers, Williams's; the person I remember was a Mr Edward and then after him came Miss Lewis, the butcher who was there for many years until Mr Williams took over. **Reg Lewis**

Beale's solicitor's office
In 1840, this was the premises of Thomas Jones, solicitor. In 1868, Arthur Cheese and George Page, solicitors, were here. In 1875 Edmund Hall Cheese took over from his brother when Arthur moved to London.

Edmund was the youngest of eight children and he and his brother Arthur were active in promoting the Golden Valley Railway. Arthur was also on the boards of the Waterworks and Gas Companies. In 1891 Edmund was deputy coroner for Herefordshire, clerk to the justices of the petty sessional divisions of Hay and Painscastle, to the commissioners of taxes for Painscastle division and to Kington highway board, commissioner for oaths and acknowledgements of deeds of married women. He was also, in his spare time, Captain of the Breconshire (1st) Volunteer Battalion, South Wales Borderers, at the Drill Hall in Lion Street.

In 1906 Henry Rowse Armstrong came to Hay as managing clerk to Mr Cheese, and married Katherine Mary Friend in 1907. She died in 1920. Her husband was found guilty of poisoning her and hanged in 1922. The present occupant of the offices, Martin Beales, wrote a book *The Hay Poisoner* attempting to prove Mr Armstrong innocent. Mr Beales has Armstrong's original office chair, and also lives in Armstrong's house in Cusop.

My mother said Mrs Armstrong wasn't the horrible person she was made out to be. My mother belonged to the Salvation Army and they used to go to the Armstrong house carol singing. Mrs Armstrong used to come to the door and see that the maid brought hot mince pies and oranges and she talked and laughed with them. She was a very jolly, nice person. My mother could never understand why she was made out to be so horrible. It's said that just before he was hung he called out his wife's name and said 'I'm coming, I'm coming'. He remonstrated bitterly that he was innocent but nobody seemed to take much notice of that. **Vera Fairfax**

ROSE AND CROWN

In 1835 Thomas James was the landlord (*Pigot's Directory*). In 1891 Thomas Stokoe ran the Rose and Crown as a family and commercial hotel. This must be the same Thomas Stokoe who was chemist, grocer, vet and maker of fizzy drinks in High Town. In 1926 George C. Barber was the landlord (*Kelly's Directory*).

The present building was originally one third longer than it is now; the present Jigsaw/Teddy Bear shop was built shortly after 1900 as an extension to the hotel accommodation. The end of the old building was pulled down to make way for it, the original beams being sawn through. There was a doorway into the present bar of the Rose and Crown from the new building, which existed until about 15 years ago, when the buildings were bought by Leon Morelli. The present Y Gelli Auctions building at the back of Y Gelli Chambers was a dance hall.

During the war, Y Gelli Chambers was used as a billet; according to Maureen the barmaid and Sara, one of the regular customers. Lily Pitt says they were G.I.s.

A couple eloping from Hay left at dead of night through gardens and down past the railway embankment to avoid the toll bridge. The hotel in which the lady worked must have been the Crown, as no other had a cook in those days. The wall from which access to the bridge was gained surrounded the garden of Charlie Williams, the stationmaster of Hay. (The last station master of Hay, Mr John, still lives in the house next to the bridge). The young couple pulled their bicycles through the bridge railings as Mr Everest the tollgate keeper slept. The elopement ended happily in Canada. **Wisps of Hay**

The Rose and Crown is a listed building, dating from the 17th century. In 1841 a party was held here to celebrate the first lighting of the gas lights in the streets of Hay, which included a procession to light all the lamps in Hay. The lamplighter was also the town crier. **Wisps of Hay**

The Amicable Friendly Society operated from here, saving for respectable funerals (a large expense in Victorian times, when funeral rituals became very complex) and providing sickness and accident insurance. It was the most superior of the three societies in Hay, having as members the vicar and Col. Powell of Hardwick. Annual celebrations comprised a procession to the church with a banner for a service, followed by dinner, which in 1843 went on till dawn. In 1840 the annual dinner of the Wyeside

Broad Street, 1901

43

Broad Street during the filming of 'Dandelion Dead'

Ploughing Association was held here at a cost of 10/- including a bottle of wine, after the ploughing match. (10/- was a week's wages for an agricultural worker).

A celebration was planned for the opening of the railway to Hay, on 19th September 1864. This was to have been held on Tump Meadow next to the Swan, but at the last minute the landlord of the Swan found out that the landlord of the Rose and Crown would be providing the refreshments, and wouldn't allow the meadow to be used. Instead, the tents of the Hereford Horticultural Society were set up in a meadow and orchard at the Nelson (now the Kingfisher). The landlord of the Rose and Crown at this time was Mr Hope, and the lunch cost 1/- a head. Mrs de Winton of Maesllwch Castle cut the sod to extend the Golden Valley railway line in 1877.

The ceremony would be followed by a public luncheon, 'to be held in a marquee at which Sir Joseph Bailey, Bart, MP, would preside'. It was also proposed to 'provide a treat for the school-children of the town and the inmates of the Workhouse'. Joint-Secretaries John Wood and Frank Holyoak signed an appeal for subscriptions. Amongst those who responded were Edmund Cheese and F.R. Trumper, solicitors, W. Webb, Hadley and Stokoe, S. Gwynne, and Penry Lloyd. Later contributors included Lord Hereford, Colonel Thomas, M. Tilley (Wheatsheaf), Reverend J.P. Powell (Llowes), P. Goodwin (Sheephouse), W. Jones (The George – later the old Post Office), W. James and T. Parry (both Hay butchers), E. Probert (The Talbot), R. Morgan (Mason's Arms), Miss Watkins (The Post Office), John Williams (The Bear), Captain Ralston (Pontywal), Fuller Maitland, MP, (Garth, Knighton) and L.R. Greene-Price (Presteigne). **Wisps of Hay**

The Rose and Crown had a mounting block.

I remember the soldiers coming to Hay during the War – G.I.s, who were also billeted at the Swan (they had sheds at the back to cook their food), the shop next to Lucinda's and the Post Office – then owned by the War Office until 1942. **Lily Pitt**

The first people I remember at the Crown was Mr Stokoe and his son. Mr Fred Stokoe was very well-known in Hay and was a reporter for the paper.

Above and overleaf: Daily Sketch reporting on the trial of 'The Hay Poisoner', local solicitor, Henry Rowse Armstrong

Page 9 DAILY SKETCH. Sun rises 8.4, sets 4.13; moon dusk to 7.17; full moon to-morrow; light lamps 4.43. THURSDAY, JANUARY 12, 1922.

NEW SENSATION IN WELSH POISON CHARGE.

"ARSENIC IN HIS POCKET."

Counsel's Sensational Statement Concerning the Arrest of Major Armstrong.

WOMEN UNDER CROSS-EXAMINATION.

Great sensation was caused just before the rising of the Hay Court yesterday, where Major Armstrong, clerk to the magistrates, is charged with attempting to murder Mr. Oswald Martin, a fellow-solicitor, by administering arsenic.

Mr. Micklethwait, counsel for the Crown, stated that when Armstrong was arrested among the contents of his pockets was found a packet containing white powder. This had been analysed, and he would prove it was a dose of white arsenic—a fatal dose.

The case proceeded more rapidly yesterday. The aged solicitor who had been acting as clerk was away and a younger man took his place.

Mrs. Gilbert Martin, who was ill after eating chocolates, and Mrs. Oswald Martin gave evidence.

MRS. MARTIN AND THE CHOCOLATES.

From Our Special Correspondent.

HAY, Wednesday: Mrs. Gilbert Martin was the first witness to-day.

She is a good-looking woman of about 30, with large dark eyes. She wore a black velvet hat with a small green plume and a dark coat, beneath which was a blue jumper and a dark green dress. A fox fur and muff completed her attire.

Her husband is a Tewkesbury corn factor, and brother of Mr. Oswald Martin.

Right away Mr. Micklethwait's examination plunged into the mystery of the chocolates.

Referring to the dinner party on October 8 at her brother-in-law's house, at which there were also present her husband, Mr. and Mrs. John Martin, and Mr. and Mrs. Oswald Martin, Mrs. Gilbert Martin said she ate some of the chocolates. She did not think any of the others had any.

About an hour after eating the chocolates she began to feel ill, and was ill throughout the night, and her heart beat very fast.

What Was Eaten at Dinner.

Mr. Matthews (cross-examining): You would not like to be certain that you were the only one to [illegible] the chocolates?—I would not like to swear it.

"I thought not," commented Mr. Matthews.

At the time you were eating the chocolates you [were] not suspicious of anything, and you were [not] attended by a doctor?—No.

[Can] you give us some idea of what you had at [the] evening meal?—Fish cakes, presumably made [of fl]our and potatoes.

[You] don't know whether it was tinned fish or [fresh] fish?—I thought it was tinned fish. We also [had] beef steak pudding, junket and cream and cheese straws. I had a glass of sherry to drink.

In reply to further questions she said she did not know at what part of the meal the wine was brought on the table.

The next witness was Mr. Gilbert Charles Martin, a young-looking man, wearing a grey suit, who corroborated his wife's account of what happened. So far as he could say, he said all at this party were in good health when they arrived there.

Another Scene.

There was a little scene between counsel when Mr. Micklethwait asked whether Mr. Gilbert Martin considered the question of calling a doctor.

"Really, I do not say it with any personal offence in the slightest," remarked Mr. Matthews, "but this is a most improper question, and I must protest."

Counsel then sat down, and the incident was about to close when Mr. Micklethwait sprang up and said, "My friend has made a most improper remark. He said I should not have introduced it unless it hurt the prisoner. I think that statement should be withdrawn. I am not here to hurt the prisoner. I am here to find out the truth."

Mr. Matthews said that if that interpretation were placed on his remarks he did withdraw them.

Mr. Martin said he did not call a doctor. He took his wife's temperature, which was 99.5 or 99.6.

[She] got up in the afternoon, and they drove to his brother's house, a few hundred yards away. She was unable to walk. She sat in the garden [for] a time; then went in and slept on the couch [till] teatime.

[M]RS. MARTIN'S STORY.

[Ate] Some of the Choco'ates and Suffered No Ill Effects.

[A] ripple of excitement ran round when Mrs. [Co]nstance Muriel Martin, wife of Mr. Oswald Norman Martin, was called.

She was smartly dressed in an electric blue toque, seal coat, and dark brown costume.

She said she met Mr. Armstrong for the first time after her engagement in 1920, being introduced to him in Mrs. Griffiths's office.

During the war she was a nurse in a hospital at [Shr]ewsbury, and later went to France to help with [a con]cert party for the entertainment of the troops.

[She] stated that for two or three months after [they h]ad changed the name of their house letters [had ar]rived addressed in the old name.

[Major] Armstrong was not in their house until [the time o]f her husband's illness.

[She re]membered a parcel coming to her husband.

"[Is] this the box?" asked Mr. Micklethwait, holding up a white cardboard box tied with green string, to which was fixed red sealing wax.

When counsel placed the box on the desk Mr. Peevor (of the Public Prosecutor's Department) opened it, and examined one of the chocolates.

Mrs. Martin identified the box by a stain on it. She also identified the salmon-coloured ribbon which she said had been tied round the box.

While Mrs. Martin was giving her evidence Major Armstrong yawned frequently, and passed his hands across his face.

Mr. Micklethwait: Did you or your husband subsequently eat any of the chocolates?—I had one or two and he had one or two. That was one evening later. Did either of you suffer any ill-effects from them?—No.

LEGAL BREEZE.

Mrs. Martin's Story of Her Husband's Illness.

The chocolates were put away until the dinner party on October 8. They were on a small dish on the table and handed round. Mrs. Gilbert Martin had one, the other people had sweets.

After the illness of her husband in October she handed the box with the remaining chocolates in it to her mother, Mrs. Davies, wife of the local chemist.

On October 26 she saw her husband after he had returned from the tea. He dictated work to his clerk. She noticed that he seemed very restless. He was looking very pale, but nothing very much. He had not his usual appetite at dinner.

Afterwards in the drawing-room he seemed restless and uncomfortable, and later he went to the bathroom and was sick.

To the best of her recollection she was present when he ran upstairs the second time.

Mr. Micklethwaite: Was he sick?—Yes, violently sick.

Mr. Matthews objected. "How can she say," he said, "whether he was sick or not. She said she was only present to the best of her recollection."

Mr. Micklethwaite: My question is perfectly proper. I don't want to keep up this wrangling.

Mrs. Martin, continuing, said that never in her nursing experience had she seen a case of this sort before.

At this stage Mr. Matthews protested that the questions were put in a leading manner.

Mr. Micklethwaite: No doubt it is a public advertisement, but I really cannot have that.

Mr. Matthews (indignantly): Public advertisement! Certainly not. It is a most improper remark.

The Chairman: The questions are a little leading.

Mr. Micklethwaite: I ought not to have made the remark about a public advertisement. It might be taken as a suggestion that my learned friend was trying to advertise himself. Of course, I don't think that at all. I withdraw my remark.

Major Armstrong smiled at the outcome of this passage between the legal representatives.

Counsel: Did you notice anything about the beating of his heart?—Yes, very, very rapid. He was shivering.

As they had not a telephone in the house a doctor was not sent for until next morning. Mr. Martin was ill for about ten days.

On the 28th Mr. Armstrong called, and was shown into the drawing-room.

Major Armstrong's Visits.

Counsel: What was the conversation?—He asked me how my husband was. I said he was better. My impression was that he seemed surprised. He then offered to do what he could for my husband, and said he would like to treat his matter as his own, as they had a good deal of business together.

Was anything said with regard to the illness of your husband?—No. He asked what was the matter, and I said we could not account for it. I thanked him for his kind offer, and afterwards he went away.

Had Mr. Armstrong been in the house on any occasion before the "at home"?—No.

Did Mr. Armstrong call again at your house?—Yes, on Sunday morning, October 30.

What did he say?—He asked how my husband was.

(Continued in Page 15.)

MAIDEN QUEEN'S "WEDDING DRESS."

Only 10 per cent. of the pupils at a well-known secondary school, when asked recently to describe Queen Elizabeth's wedding dress, mentioned that she never married. The other 90 per cent. answered the question with more or less elaborate detail.

MEN SANDY LIKES.

Pure Cockney Always a Good Pal and Never a Shirker.

LOVED THE DEVONIANS.

It is curious how the Scots take so readily to some Englishmen in preference to others.

I have interviewed scores of ex-service men (writes a correspondent to the *Daily Sketch*), including a colonel of a Highland regiment, and they have nearly all told the same story of having such a preference.

Devonshire men have always been good pals with Scots. I do not know if it is because Devonshire, of all the counties in England, resembles Scotland more than any other in England.

True as Steel.

An old regular soldier—a Gordon—says he has been brigaded with the Devons very often; fought side by side with them, and always found them "true as steel."

But perhaps the Scot's love for the unadulterated Cockney is the strangest of all. In France over and over again a London Cockney was the life of the billet. He never groused at extras, was always a good pal, and never a shirker.

The typical Londoner the Scots never took to, and the Welsh they had no overwhelming love for. On the other hand, they liked the sturdy men from Cornwall, and made good chums with the Tynesiders.

Lancashire Men A1.

Manchester men they could not stick, but men from the county of Lancashire were found A1.

"Yorkies" were almost as good as the Devon men, and Liverpool "blokes" made good pals.

It would be interesting to know the type of Scotsmen Englishmen favour most.

WHEN THE PIGS FLY

Pork Will be High and Women Will Sit in Parliament!

Many an old saw contains the germ of a great truth, but who would suspect a nursery jingle to be prophetic and for the prophecy to be fulfilled to the letter?

A *Daily Sketch* reader calls attention to the picture published a few days ago of a pig in an aeroplane and recalls a rhyme of childhood days:

When the pigs begin to fly,
Oh, won't the pork be high!
They'll have old women in Parliament
When the pigs begin to fly.

"Now," she writes, "we live to see the prophecy come true. The price of pork is most certainly high, and women are in Parliament"—not, however, *old* ones.

Could someone supply the origin of the jingle?

Very Unlikely Birds.

One doesn't exactly know how that pig flew to the Continent the other day. He should go tail first to make another old jingle true.

Pigs might fly, but they're very unlikely birds.
Pigs when they fly go tail first.

It is unnecessary to quote some of the old saws about the pig to show their truth. One will suffice: "Pigs grow fat where lambs would starve."

English and French proverbs about the cat in the bag and the pig in a poke are closely associated. The French say "Acheter chat en poche"—a reference to substituting a cat for a sucking-pig and trying to palm it off on greenhorns. If anyone bought the article and opened the sack for examination he let "the cat out of the bag," and the trick was disclosed. The French "chat en poche" refers to the fact, while the English proverb regards the trick.

ZOO FLAPPER'S FAST.

Takes a Meal Now Quite Satisfied All is Well.

A flap-necked chameleon is among the most interesting of the latest additions to the Zoo. The reptile is keeping company with a Senegal and a common chameleon.

It had refused to take any food for two or three weeks prior to its arrival at the Zoo, but yesterday it was prevailed upon by Keeper Collins to make a substantial meal off some luscious cockchafers.

It is a striking-looking creature in light and dark shades of grey and brown, and was the more interesting to visitors by reason of its restlessness.

Owing no doubt to a desire not to be caught napping, its eyes seem to be constantly looking all ways at once. While one of them is gazing up the other is looking down; at another time one eye is to be seen glancing suspiciously backwards, and the other looking with equal furtiveness forward.

False Alarm.

When this chameleon arrived it was a bright yellow. This gave Collins some concern, for, as he says, "they turn that colour when they are going to die." The unlucky hue, however, soon changed to a more auspicious one, and the keeper breathed a deep sigh of relief.

Mr. M. Brother, Textile Workers' Union, will be Labour candidate for Duddeston, Birmingham.

FREE TRIP TO LONDON AND £10 CHEQUE.

Privileges of Dancers Who Take Part in Big Contest.

CHANCE IN THE FINAL.

Notts Couples Invade Derby and Carry Away Prizes.

Would you like to win a £10 cheque and a free trip to London?

You may do both, and also compete for a further £700 in the final, if you enter the *Daily Sketch* £1,500 National Amateur Dancing Competition.

So far three district contests have been held—two in London and one in the provinces—and interest is growing keener every day.

At Derby on Tuesday night many Nottingham dancers, who made a special journey, took [part] and all the four prizes went to that town.

The Winners at Derby.

Miss Hilda Barnes, 60, Moffat-street, Nottingham, and Mr. Harry Green, 18, Mell[ors]-street, Corporation-road, Nottingham, won the valse, and Miss B. Richardson, 76, Woodborough-road, Nottingham, and Mr. C. H. Cornell, 12, Egerton-street, St. Anne's Hill-road, Nottingham, the fox-trot.

Cheques for £10 were handed to these four winners at the conclusion of the contest.

To-night the second provincial contest takes place at the Coliseum, Southampton. Dancing will take place from 7.30 until midnight.

Mr. Russell Kaye, Southsea, Miss [illegible], Southampton, and Mr. Timmins, Bournemouth, all well-known experts, will be the judges.

To-morrow night another contest will be held at the Colston Hall, Bristol, from 7.30 until midnight.

At all the district contests there will be plenty of dancing for those who do not wish to enter the competition.

Next Week's Competitions.

Next week's contests are:—

London.—Wednesday: Mile End People's Palace. Tickets 2s. 6d.

Bradford.—Tuesday: Windsor Hall. Tickets 2s. 6d.

Liverpool.—Thursday: St. George's Hall. Tickets 2s. 6d.

Manchester.—Friday: White City Ballroom. Tickets 2s. 6d.

Leeds.—Friday: Victoria Hall. Tickets 2s. 6d.

Brighton.—Friday: Sherry's. Tickets 5s.

Cardiff.—Friday: City Hall. Tickets 5s.

Whitley Bay.—Saturday: Empress Ballroom. Tickets 2s. 6d.

Tickets are on sale at the *Daily Sketch* office[s], London and Manchester and Liverpool, at the ha[lls], or the local secretaries of the National Insti[tute] for the Blind.

WOMAN DAY BY D[AY].

A Pneu Disease.—"My husband is a[ll] ammonia," said an applicant at Maryl[ebone] [illegible]

Artistic Language.—"She called [illegible] names when I spoke to her husban[d]," [said a] woman at Acton. Process was granted f[or] language.

Jewelled Picture of Princess.—An album, [which] included a hand-painted picture of Princess [Mary] set with jewels, and which contains the nam[es of] the visitors resident at the Piccadilly Hotel on N[ew] Year's Eve, was sent to Princess Mary by th[e] youngest resident, Miss Dennis, aged seven.

"Loveless and Unhappy."—A Windermere girl, Sarah Jane Bugdale, was awarded £50 damages and costs at Lancaster against Arthur Pop, of Bolton, for breach of promise. The wedding was fixed for last June, guests were invited, and rooms taken for the honeymoon. Pop then wrote saying the marriage could only be loveless and unhappy.

Jewish Bride.—Miss Winifred Van Noorden, only daughter of Mr. Alfred Van Noorden, managing director of the Carl Rosa Opera Company, was married at the Jewish Synagogue, St. John's Wood, yesterday afternoon, to Capt. W. M. Goodman, M.C., of Plymouth, according to the picturesque ritual of the Jewish faith, to which both parties belong. The bride, who was given away by her father, was attended by eight bridesmaids, four being members of her family and four members of the bridegroom's family, and the service was conducted by the Rev. H. Price, stepfather of the bridegroom.

THINGS PEOPLE SAY.

Virtue cannot be picked up cheaply like a bargain at a January sale.—Father Degen.

The silver sea is no longer our first line of defence; it can be more truly described as the last ditch.—Prof. Vilden-Hart.

The canker of ca'canny has been created (by the eight hours day), and is gnawing at our vitals.—Mr. D. A. Mathéson, general manager, Caledonian Railway.

We promise to work hand in hand with our fellow-citizens for the prosperity of the island that never oppressed a suffering nation.—Jews of Cork to President Griffith.

He belonged to a local dance band run by Mr Rees Harding, who was the church organist. They were two well-known characters.

I remember the Crown being opened and the Stokoe family being there and I can also remember a man who looked after the horses, a fellow called George Fawcett. People used to bring their horses – you see in the old days before they had the mechanised fire engine the horses who pulled the carriages from the Crown used to (and I can't remember this but I remember the older folks saying) pull the fire engine and were kept over Hay Bridge on the other side of the river. When the fire call came they would open the gates and the horses would automatically run to the fire station on their own; they were quite used to the job. I knew this because not only had my parents said about it but I was also in the fire service for 25 years. **Reg Lewis**

Y Gelli Auctions was the ballroom of the Crown. They used to have dances there. It was a lovely ballroom. That's where they used to have all the wedding receptions because Ann, my daughter, got married and I had her reception there. The Crown was a lovely hotel. **Emma Dunn**

I was born in 1924, went into the army in 1942, came back in 1946 and worked in the shop until 1983. I count myself fortunate to have lived in Hay all my life.

We had a dramatic society; the problem with it was that we didn't have a big enough hall; we used the Parish Hall and the ballroom at the Crown, and we started a campaign to get a grant to raise money for a public hall. I can remember a councillor who said it was a waste of time because there were five places in Hay, but none of them would hold more than forty people. Our campaign came to nothing because grants were stopped. We used to go to Builth Wells, Brecon and Talgarth and put on our plays. The most successful was one called 'The Wishing Well', which was a Welsh comedy, and I reckon it would be popular even now. We did 'The Young Mrs Barrington', 'Journey's End', all sorts. We used to rely on the young bank clerks — because Hay had a limited population, it was hard to get people to take part, but the bank clerks were always changing and we had some brilliant young people. **Tony Pugh**

THE SEVEN STARS, 11 BROAD STREET

This is a listed building, probably dating from the 17th century. It was licensed as a pub before 1776 and had grazing rights on the common. In 1835 the landlord was John Sheen (*Pigot's Directory*), in 1891 Phillip Clarke and in 1926 Robert Williams.

12 BROAD STREET

This is another listed building, probably dating from the 17th century. In 1926 Frank Cadman, JP and corn merchant, lived here. He also owned the town flour mills.

There was a corn merchant next to the Seven Stars, Cadmans. **Emma Dunn**

TINTO HOUSE, 13 BROAD STREET

This is another listed building, dating from the early to mid-18th century. In the 1920s, Dr T.S.H. Hinks practiced from here before he retired. He died in 1930, aged 85. His son Tom continued to practice medicine from here until his death in 1932.

On the day the verdict was due Dr Hinks, painfully aware of the fact that he would lose all credibility in the town, was prepared for the worst. Having testified against Armstrong, he knew that a 'Not Guilty' verdict would be his downfall. He had therefore arranged to sell his practice to a Dr Lamb, but had not yet signed the contract.

On that fateful day, he sat at a table in Tinto House, the unsigned contract in front of him. The telephone rang. The conversation over, he laid the receiver to rest with a deep sigh of relief. The verdict was 'Guilty'. Armstrong would hang. Dr Hinks tore up the contract. Dr Lamb never did get a practice in Hay, although he returned to the area after his retirement and eventually died in the Mid Wales Hospital, Talgarth. **John Evans**

14 BROAD STREET

The doctor's surgery was where Rose's bookshop is.
Emma Dunn

15 BROAD STREET

The other wallpaper shop was in that music shop by the Clock Tower. Edgar Evans's grandfather had that and of course he was the chief fireman in Hay, volunteer service as it is today. Edgar Evans's grandfather started all that and his father was in it.
Emma Dunn

Brian Wiggington had his shop where the music shop is now, and before the Red Cross shop was there.
Gordon and Jennifer Lawrence

The building is now Hancock and Monks music shop.

THE GRANARY, 16 BROAD STREET

This is also a listed building. It was formerly a wool store and may later have been part of the large U-shaped complex incorporating the former agricultural hall in Lion Street (now Booths). It dates from the early 19th century and is shown on the 1847 tithe map. It is now a café.

The Granary was a grain merchant. It belonged to Nigel Birch's grandfather. He used to deal in corn and what have you and Cadmans the other side of the road. **Emma Dunn**

GOLESWORTHY'S, 17 BROAD STREET

In 1891 this was the shop of Frank Woodland Golesworthy, outfitter and boot factor *(Kelly's Directory)*. It is a listed building dating from the early 19th century, and is shown on the 1847 tithe map. The Victorian alterations may date from 1883, when the shop was established.

Mr Dan Davies, who is the grandfather of Peter and Michael and all the others of the Like family, managed the business for us for many years. He would have managed the business from 1900 when the family returned to Cheltenham until he died in 1926 and I know the date; it stuck in my memory because my dad had taken me down to the river. Those times the outdoor recreations were still a going concern. There was no such thing as going off to a skating rink – you skated on the ponds locally and so we went down to the river because there was ice on the river. Eric Evans was down there skating and said to me 'Come on' and I stood on his skates and he took me all over the river. I thought that was wonderful. So when we'd finished and we're walking back to Hay – there's a little track across the Warren and as we came to the track Jack Lewis was coming down. Of course he worked in the shop as well and he met Dad and he said Mr Dan Davies had died.

Well, from then on, as far as our business was concerned, my father and brother ran it until I took over the business in 1970 and I retired I think in 1985 and my son is there now. **Roger Golesworthy**

Golesworthys weren't as big as they are now, because it only went to the shop that's right on the corner. The other two windows they've got was a separate tailors. He would measure people up for suits and that. Well, Golesworthys didn't do that. They did shoes but they didn't do children's clothes or anything. Pugh's was a much bigger shop than Golesworthys. The bottom two windows of Golesworthys were Jones the tailors and they sold shoes and they measured people as well. **Emma Dunn**

BARCLAYS BANK

This is another listed building, with a Victorian frontage on an earlier structure. The first bank on this site is thought to have started in 1850, though there is a gravestone in Hay Churchyard to the manager of the Herefordshire Banking Co., Rees Howells, dated April 1845. The company was formed in Hereford in 1836. In 1850 the manager was Bernard Matthews, who was followed by J.T. Bowen. The bank failed in June 1863 and the branch was bought by the Bank of Wales and re-opened a month later. However, in 1864 it closed again. In 1883 the Birmingham, Dudley and District Banking Co., opened with Alline Bushell as the manager. He also lived in Broad Street.

In 1889 the name changed to the Birmingham District and Counties Banking Co., amalgamating with the Wolverhampton and Staffordshire Banking Co. Ltd. In 1907 it became the United Counties Bank, and in 1917 it became Barclays Bank.

In 1926 the manager was William Owen Price, who was also treasurer of the Urban District Council, treasurer of the Cusop and Eardisley parish councils and treasurer of the Hay and Talgarth school district. He lived at Bank House, next door to the bank.

SOUTH BANK HOUSE, 18 BROAD STREET

Originally known as Bank House, it was built in 1790, and is a listed building. The bank bought the property in 1853, and the manager's office is still in the house. However, according to *Kelly's Directory*, the occupants in 1891 were George and Charles Butcher, coal, lime, manure and seed merchants. In 1926, though, the manager of the bank, William Owen Price, lived here.

....and Mr Wop Price the Bank, always referred to as Wop because his initials were W-O-P. **Reg Lewis**

PROSPECT HOUSE, 20 BROAD STREET

This is also known as Chancery House, and is a listed building, dated 1775 and initialled S.P. Information about this building is rather confusing. In *Kelly's Directory* for 1891 the occupant is listed as William Byron, woolstapler and agent for the Breconshire Coal and Lime Company Ltd, and William Terrett. In 1926 the occupant was Thomas Price.

MONTPELIER HOUSE, 21 BROAD STREET

This is a listed building with a later 19th-century front. It is now a bookshop.

22 BROAD STREET

This is a listed building with a later 19th-century front, and 17th-century origins. It was originally part of West House, and was later altered to match No. 21. The interior retains a studded partition wall, now dividing this property from West House, but originally an internal division. It has been a succession of bookshops in the last few years, including The Poetry Bookshop (twice), the Penguin Bookshop, and part of West House Bookshop.

WEST HOUSE, BROAD STREET

This is a listed building which originated as a 17th-century timber-frame structure, with 21 Broad Street being a rebuild of the former cross range. It was rebuilt in stone in the later 18th century, perhaps at the same time as adjoining properties. In 1858 it was a malthouse. It is now a bookshop.

SYCAMORE HOUSE, 24 BROAD STREET

This listed building dates from the mid- to late 18th century, and is said to have been built at the same time as Brynhyfred next door. It housed the Mechanic's Institute in the mid-19th century, including a library and reading room. Some of the books were given to the library by Thomas Phillips, a surgeon apprenticed to an apothecary in Hay. The Institute was formed in April 1842. There were annual dinners (at the Rose and Crown across the road). The library closed in 1849, but was revived in 1851 as the Hay Library Institution thanks to Rev Bevan. By 1861 the library had 70 members, and held fortnightly lectures on a wide variety of subjects. This, too, closed in the 1870s. Francis Kilvert mentions attending a Book Club Sale in November 1871, which may have been the sale of the defunct library's stock.

In 1891 the master of the British School, Thomas E. James, lived here, and by 1926 he had become a local magistrate. **Kelly's Directory**

....then Mr and Mrs Davies. Miss Davies later became Mrs J.V. Like from the Garage. **Reg Lewis**

It was named after the sycamore that grew in its garden. **Karl Showler**

BRYNHYFRED, 25 BROAD STREET

This is a listed building, which is said to have been built about 1775. Wilson's the dentist was next door.

WYE VIEW

In 1926 James M. Brookes, dentist, worked here on Thursdays from 9am to 4pm.

25A is a Victorian rebuild of the former coach house to Brynhyfred. As both buildings are considerably above the present road surface, and there is no back way into the property, there must have been a ramp. This can be seen in the cobbled surface immediately in front of 25A, cut off by the later paving of the area in front of the cottages next door. **Kelly's Directory**

26 BROAD STREET

In 1891 Thomas Evans lived here. Mr and Mrs Elkington lived in one of the cottages set back behind the cobbles and on market days Mrs Elkington couldn't get the push chair out over the cobbles.

The market was in Broad Street until 1956, though the sheep and cattle moved away before then. **Kelly's Directory**

27 BROAD STREET

In 1891, Mrs Watkins lived here. **Kelly's Directory**

31 - 32 BROAD STREET

In 1887 this was a pub called the Tanner's Arms, which served the nearby tannery on Broad Street. In 1891 Edwin Hathaway was the landlord.

The Old Tanners Arms was a well-known fish shop for years and Mr Martin Jones used to run it. **Kelly's Directory**

POPLAR HOUSE, BROAD STREET

This is a listed building, on the corner of Heol-y-dwr. It was formerly called Pound Head, in the early 19th century, though the present building is mid-19th century, and is shown on the 1847 tithe map.

In 1891 Miss Mary Stephens was a dressmaker here (quite a high class one, from the size of the property). In 1926 Charles Jones lived here. It is now divided up into studio flats.

Nigel Birch's mother used to live in that big house opposite Underhills garage. It's now made in flats. That's where his mother and father lived, and his grandfather. His father worked in a bank in Hay – in Barclays. **Emma Dunn**

NEWPORT STREET – (A CONTINUATION OF BROAD STREET)

A list of public houses was published in the book *Wisps of Hay:*

Ship (J. Smith), The Lamb (un-named), Bridge-End (G.A. Lage). There were the following pubs between The Nelson (now the Kingfisher guest house) and the Town Clock:

The Nelson

The Bridge (now Celtic Canoes)

The Lamb (now the vet's)

The Ship (now demolished - waste ground next to the Globe Gallery)

The Tanners Arms (afterwards a fish and chip shop, now Mary Fields' house)

The Three Tuns

The Black Swan

One opposite West House

The Crown

The Seven Stars

The King's Head (Tredegar House)

If you came up from the railway station, opposite the station was the Nelson Inn, which is now the Kingfisher, then you come up to the vet's on the right-hand side, there was the Lamb, then higher up by the garage there was one I can't remember but it was open before my time; the Tanner's Arms, then there was the Three Tuns, which is open still, and the other side was the Black Swan, which is next to the steak bar, or bookshop as it is now, and of course the Seven Stars, and just to the left of the town clock was the King's Head, next door to what's now the public toilets. **Reg Lewis**

The farmer in Cusop, where he moved to, used to supply milk and would take it down to the station at 7.45am every day on a horse-drawn cart. He used to tear down the road and just about caught the train

by having the horses go at full gallop through the town.

Timber wagons used to come through the town, drawn by two or three horses, and the timber was so heavy that when they were going downhill they used to put wedges under the wheels to stop the cart running into the horses. **Mac Maddy**

There was the Congregational chapel opposite Mr Underhill's garage – it was the United Reform Church for a while. **Reg Lewis**

There was a Sunday School attached to the Ebenezer Chapel around 1902. The Sunday School teachers seem to have been Ivy W. Gibbs, a Castle Street draper, and William James McCarthy, a tailor with Septimus Williams, also in Castle Street. He came from Kinross. The Sunday School superintendant was Mr Walton. **Wisps of Hay**

Brian Wiggington used to have his workshop under what is now The Globe Gallery. **Jennifer and Gordon Lawrence**

The Nelson was dry during the war on a Sunday. Everybody on a Sunday used to go to the Oak, which is Hardwicke way. They couldn't open the Nelson although it was in England and then they went to court and decided, yes, they could open it. The Welsh pubs stayed dry. I was in the Nelson once before I was married and someone said to me 'Emma, your *mother's coming down Ship Pitch." I had to go all the way round Roderick's Lane over the fields to Bear Street to get home before she found out. She hated pubs – and smoking.* **Emma Dunn**

HEOL-Y-DWR – JUST OFF BROAD STREET

Lily Pitt used to play in the street as a child – there were no cars, only horses and carts as there was a brook that crossed the road so it wasn't suitable for cars.

Electricity only came to Hay in about 1925 and it was then generated in a power station behind Brook House in Heol-y-dwr. It wasn't strong enough for many people to use it so they relied on gas until mains electricity came in 1932, supplied by Shropshire, Worcestershire and Staffordshire Power Company. Mr W. Elson had owned the power station so he sold out to them and became their manager, with an office in Kington. However, few people bothered with it until after the war. **Dick Elkington**

According to **Wisps of Hay,** Bill Lilwall, county court bailiff and Salvation Army member, introduced electricity to Hay.

Where I live now, Garth Felin, was originally a Napoleonic grain barn. During the Napoleonic War, this country was blockaded, so we had to start storing the grain and several of these were built. When I first saw it, before it was converted, I said 'No way. I'm not going to live there,' but when it was finished it was lovely. **Vera Fairfax**

CASTLE STREET

Castle Street seems to have been the part of Hay where the gentry chose to live in the earlier part of the 19th century, and also a popular location for small private schools.

In the *Pigot and Co Directory* of 1835, members of the gentry living in Castle Street were listed as Mrs Grimes, and Capt Irwin. In 1830 E. and F. Powell had a girls' boarding school here, which had moved to Oxford Road by 1835. In 1835, according to *Pigot's Directory,* the Rev Thomas Phillips ran a gentleman's boarding school while his wife or sister Mary Phillips ran a ladies' boarding school. George Edge ran a boarding and day school in 1844, and in 1846 G.T. Heslop ran a Commercial Academy and boarding school. The exact locations of these schools are not known, unlike those of others in Castle Street.

Shops in Castle Street were:

John Harper, baker and flour dealer
William Willmot, baker and confectioner
Edmund Bissell, bookseller, stationer and
    book binder
John Wilson, bookseller, bookbinder, printer
    and stationer
Roger Maskell and William Parry, boot and
    shoe makers
William James, butcher
Thomas Hooper, chemist, druggist, grocer and
    dealer in sundries
Henry Bridgewater and William Powell, coal and
    lime merchants
John Llewellyn, cooper

William Herrietts, glass and earthenware dealer
Ann Powell, glass and earthenware dealer and
*   grocer, dealer in sundries and tallow chandler*
Eliza Probert, grocer and dealer in sundries
John Francis, hairdresser
Elizabeth Lewis, milliner and dressmaker
James Watkins, saddler
John Williams, stone mason
Elizabeth Higgins and Ann Howells, straw hat
*   makers*
James Lyde, surgeon
Thomas Howells, tailor
Thomas Williams, beer retailer

…mention must be made of the street name-signs to be encountered during these walks. Made of cast iron, most of those in the town centre date from the 1870s when the streets were renamed. The contract to make these was first given to Eastwood, a local ironfounder, but when it was realised that as a member of the awarding board he was ineligible the contract was transferred to Robert Williams and Son. **Walking Round Hay**

Reg Lewis lived at Ardens at one time and George House was the George Hotel. **Dick Elkington**

Royal George – sited almost opposite the Blue Boar and not at the Vicarage as is generally supposed. **Wisps of Hay**

THE CASTLE

The section of the boundary wall to Hay Castle, with the entrance to the Castle Gardens (now also the Honesty Bookshop) is listed. It may have been built by Sir Joseph Bailey after he purchased the castle in 1844. He was the Lord of the Manor and responsible for the running of the weekly market.

I knew the caretaker at the castle and used to get her shopping for her. The castle was gorgeous in those days, with beautiful grounds and furniture that was 'out of this world'. There was a carpet with a coat of arms. I think Lady Glanusk lived there then.

My father used to say 'Don't swing on those railings (by the castle gates) because Bramwell Bradley will come down and frighten you. Well, one day when it was getting a bit late, about half past eight and beginning to get dark, and we were playing there, when all of a sudden the gates were wide open and this chap came floating down the drive with a sheet over him! It was Bramwell, who was a sort of odd job man at the castle and was a bit strange. The fire at the castle was 'a terrible affair'. **Mona Morgan**

Mary Davies remembers being taken to see the castle when it was on fire (this would have been the 1939 fire).

The castle itself was very private in those days, you daren't walk up the drive, you know. You wouldn't even think of walking up the driveway. It was owned by a man by the name of Mr Choose. He belonged to the fairground people. **Brian Wilding**

I remember Richard Booth coming to town and buying up all the empty shops, though he had to sell them again when he he had problems. He was full of himself in those days. He bought the castle for £2,000. **Eleri Golesworthy**

When we came back in 1976 the bookshop business was starting to expand. The gentleman at the castle was allocating people to do various jobs. Someone told him that I was a precision engineer. He said 'It's not paid.' I said 'Well, please yourself'. The initial change to me is it's a good thing for visitors but I'm not sure the locals are quite so keen. **Charlie Evans**

1 CASTLE STREET

Miss Agnes Beavan, dressmaker lived here, with her brother or husband Edwin, who was a tailor, in 1891. It is now Lucinda's hairdressers. *(Kelly's Directory).*

This was Mrs Hamer's sweet shop. **Dick Elkington**

Mrs Hamer did faggots and peas. **Emma Dunn**

There were two more grocers in Castle Street; one was part of a group called 'Maypole' run by Mr Williams but I can't remember the other one. I think they were at Lucinda's and the print shop. **Eleri Golesworthy**

Hay Castle in 1830

2 CASTLE STREET

This was Keylocks the butchers with its own slaughter house. This is now Forwood's print shop. It had a well in the yard.

Keylocks had ten children. If they only earned a shilling it was something in those days. Keylocks had a slaughterhouse at the side of there. You could hear them shooting the cattle on a Monday. Buy them on a Monday and sometimes shoot them on a Monday and have them in the shop next day. **Emma Dunn**

They remember doing a round and everyone would close their shops and go and eat at his shop – all the children had to do these meat rounds.
Derek Addyman

MANCHESTER HOUSE, 3 CASTLE STREET

In 1891 George Watkins was a monumental mason and sculptor here, and in 1926 Arthur Evans, butcher, had his shop here Until recently it was Castle China. Now it is Number Two (clothing shop), with bed and breakfast accommodation above. *(Kelly's Directory).*

A few yards further on, 'Castle China' displays two delightful carved stone panels depicting fruit and birds... **Walking Round Hay**

...and then Dougie Williams. It was a tailor's shop where they measured up. **Emma Dunn**

LEICESTER HOUSE, CASTLE STREET

This never had a street number, but is between 3 and 4. Originally, it was a single storey stone building, but had a red brick façade and upper floor added in the late 19th or early 20th century. It is now Focus clothes shop.

4 CASTLE STREET

In 1891 Henry Thomas Lewis, tailor, lived here *(Kelly's Directory).* It is now the baker's and Wye Café.

The bread shop was Rosie Wright's fruit and veg shop. **Dick Elkington**

The shop next to Focus was a greengrocer's too, where Harris's is. **Emma Dunn**

Harris's – he remembers his mum selling faggots and peas from the back of his place too, a little café there. He said it was like the fast food of that time. **Derek Addyman**

Well, faggots and peas were lovely. **Emma Dunn**

5 CASTLE STREET

This was the Dog Inn, later renamed The Talbot. A talbot was a breed of hunting dog, now extinct. It had a licence before 1776. In 1835 the landlord was James Price *(Pigot's Directory).* In 1891 the landlord was Llewellyn Lewis and in 1899 it had a seven day licence. It is now Wye Gallery Prints.

...Hay Prints with its restored carved and painted corbels. **Walking Round Hay**

That was Lloyds the chemist. **Emma Dunn**

This was a chemist's but before that it was another pub, the Dog. **Dick Elkington**

Part of the shop opposite Spar where Mrs Annie Grant had her toy shop and where there's a print shop next door there was a pub in those days called The Talbot,

but all the locals called it The Dog, though I don't know why. The gent who kept it was Charlie Walters who was the local billposter around the town, used to put anything that was going on in town, or sales.
Reg Lewis

GRANT'S NEWSAGENTS, 6 CASTLE STREET

This is a listed building, which includes the former Flannel Mill to the rear. It is shown on the 1847 tithe map, but the frontage dates to about 1860, with the flannel mill being early 19th century. It was converted into a printing house when the front was rebuilt, and this was closed in 1956. In 1987 the former mill was largely disused, but it has now been converted into flats.

At the end of the 18th century Thomas Howells set up a spinning and weaving manufactory in the flannel mill. It employed 70-80 people, mainly carding and spinning wool and weaving linseys (wool/linen mix) and coarse woollen cloth for miners' shirts in South Wales. Unable to compete with later steam powered mills, by 1868 it was 'almost extinct', according to Geoffrey Fairs. This would be when it was converted into a printing works.

Clearly there was no possibility of using water-power here and it is almost certain that hand-powered machinery was used for most of the mill's operating life. **Walking Round Hay**

Thomas Howells was a prominent Quaker, and the father of Susannah Swetman, who, with her father, had an interest in 4 High Town, the Quaker meeting house.

In 1808 Howells travelled to America but although he was offered substantial inducements to establish mills in Pennsylvania he returned to Hay, dying in 1819, to be buried in the churchyard, described as 'a woollen manufacturer of this town'. **Walking Round Hay**

In 1848, William Harris started the first printing here, and three years later the business was taken over by George Horden. He was the deputy to the Superintendent Registrar as well as being bookseller, stationer and printer. He also managed the Savings Bank (branch of Brecon Savings Bank), which was open on Thursdays from 12 noon to 1pm.

In 1891 Henry Richard Grant took over, followed by his son, John Grant, who gradually ran down the printing side of the business. He was succeeded by his son, also John Grant, who died in 1998. The younger John Grant caught the 'Best Armadillo in the 1982 Season' (he was something of a practical joker), which he displayed in his window.

In 1926 John Grant obtained permission from the Catholic Bishop of Menevia for mass to be said in his house at Castle Street, and later the upper room of the Cheese Market was used, until the Catholic congregation acquired their own church in Belmont Road.

…both Grant's (Newsagents) and Steve Davies' (Electrical) have their windows divided by delicate arched or decorated pillars. Notice, too, the little moulded plaster ceiling in the entrance to Anne Grant's sweetshop. **Walking Round Hay**

Grants used to do printing, the printer being a man called Godfrey Turner, who still lives in Hay. **Dick Elkington**

I worked in Grants when I first left school at fourteen. I think I got three shillings a week. John Grant's grandma, she was a wonderful lady. She was like Queen Victoria to look at, her hair all up. She was lovely, and the grandfather, he was lovely too. My brother and Mr Clayton, they worked in the print shop. That place that goes back used to be all china, everything. Right back there were loads and loads of shelves of china and they sold toys. They never ever sold sweets like they do now [up until its closure in 2001]. **Emma Dunn**

7 CASTLE STREET

In 1891 John Bevan, watch maker and jeweller, lived here *(Kelly's Directory)*. Then it became Steve Davies Domestic Appliances (Steve Davies retired in late 1999).

The last three shops were all owned by a Mr Moxon, the first being a photographer's, the second had sweets and tobacco and the third toys and fancy goods. **Dick Elkington**

Where Mayalls is used to be the haberdashery shop, Moxons. Steve Davies was there before Mayalls. **Emma Dunn**

8 CASTLE STREET

The next shop used to be a sweet shop. **Emma Dunn**

9 CASTLE STREET

In 1891 Thomas Kinsey had a grocers' and stationers' shop here *(Kelly's Directory)*. Now Bags of Books, it was previously the SWALEC office. When SWALEC announced the closure of their office, over 900 signatures were collected on a petition of protest within hours of the announcement. They put a phone line into the SPAR shop instead.

…and the end shop, a bookshop now, used to be a toy shop. It all belonged to Moxons. It used to be the electricity shop. **Emma Dunn**

10 CASTLE STREET, THE PENNY BUN

The Grapes (Gittins). **Wisps of Hay**

There was a well in the garden of the Penny Bun and wells all over town. **Mac Maddy**

Alf Gittins had a grocer's in one half of W.H. Jones and the Wye Hotel. **Dick Elkington**

That's where I went to work and they used to do weddings there because they had a very big room which Wendy's got now at the back (in Jones's hardware shop) and they used to call it the Market Room and they had Jones's as well. That's where I first got interested in hotel work. Everybody said Mrs Gittins was a slavedriver but I found she never asked you to do anything she couldn't do and she worked with you. I mean, I've worked there until ten o'clock at night, perhaps getting a table ready for a wedding or something, but she was always there with you. Her mother, old Mrs Hitchcock, always made sure, no matter how busy you were, that you had a good meal. Very important. She'd say, 'Now come on, you girls. I got it ready, now come and eat it,' and you always had the best meal you could have there. Old Mrs Hitchcock was wonderful.

Commercial travellers stayed there and it was a nice hotel. It was all commercial, no tourists. I mean, Hay wasn't on the market. Nobody'd heard of Hay. It wasn't Hay-on-Wye then, just Hay and people used to call it Welsh Hay. My Dad worked in England and came home for his lunch in Wales, over the border.
Emma Dunn

12 CASTLE STREET

This was originally The Cock, which was licenced before 1776. In 1815 it became the office for the tramroad.

The present ironmonger's shop was, in the early 19th century, the offices of the Hay Railway Company operating the horse-drawn tramway from Brecon to Eardisley.... A small recess at a height of about 8 feet, in the wall of this building is the only evidence left of the Town Gate once on this site. **Walking Round Hay**

In 1891 John Jones was a boot and shoe maker here, followed in 1926 by William Edwards. *(Kellys Directory)*. It is now W.H. Jones' hardware shop.

Mona Morgan was born in Swansea, her father working for the nickel works at Clydach. He was gassed whilst working there and they moved to 12 Castle Street when Mona was three or four years old, her grandparents already having lived there for years. Her grandfather made shoes, her father then becoming a photographer, taking pictures of weddings, and opened a shop called Edwards. Prior to her grandparents having the place it was a pub called the White Cock of which there was an emblem painted on one of the bedroom doors.

One day my father put his foot through one of the floorboards and he got a light and looked into the hole that had been made, and he could see a room. He took up a bit more of the floorboard and you could see a small round room, all covered in dust, with stone walls and an old, old door. He said he was going to get a ladder and go down there one day but shortly after that he had a stroke and died at the early age of 53, so it was as though it wasn't meant to be. My mother had the hole covered up after that.
Mona Morgan

Mona Morgan described a 'socket' on the front wall of W.H. Jones – something to do with Cromwell coming to the gates of Hay and she thought the vicar would know more.

We had an outside toilet big enough to have the mangle in it, and there was a door that led into a cellar in which poachers once hid from the police. There was another door inside that room, so perhaps it was to a cellar belonging to the pub. There were pigs kept at the end of the garden – most people kept a pig in those days. **Mona Morgan**

Wendy Jones, that used to be Hitchcocks. One part of her shop used to be Hitchcocks and then it was Gittins and of course Mrs Gittins was a Hitchcock and they used to have it and then they ran that commercial hotel, [now the Penny Bun].
Emma Dunn

13 CASTLE STREET

Mona Morgan remembers Boz Books before it was the fire station, as just a derelict building that she and other children used to play in. The fire engines were kept at the back of the castle, and Edgar Evans was the Chief Officer.

When I was in the fire service we'd been moved from Castle Lane and the fire station was opposite the Blue Boar. It's a bookshop now. Of course, first of all there was a tractor, which pulled the fire engine, then it came to a lorry and that was the stage where I came in. We had the lorry pull it for a long time and of course then it came to an old Dennis open fire engine, which was stood on the fire engine and then eventually they got the modern one, which is more or less the same as they have today. I was with the fire service when they moved up to the Brecon Road on September 28th 1957. We had a celebration at the fire station and it was my wedding anniversary and I should have got home but I didn't get there till midnight. That didn't go down very well! We had very many chimney fires and things like that, but of course we had the bigger fires like Hay Castle.
Reg Lewis

Mary Davies remembers they wanted to put a siren for the fire station on her family's chimney, but her father put his foot down; he said it would wake the children! So they put up some scaffolding at the back.

14 CASTLE STREET

In 1891 George Wood was a greengrocer at this address, and in 1926 William Evans was a boot and shoe repairer. It now houses a hairdresser's, and is a listed building. *(Kelly's Directory).*

Mary Davies was born here. Her father ran a cobbler's shop.

Mrs Thomas, who ran the Blue Boar, was the midwife, so only had to come across the street to deliver me. I wasn't allowed out much to play as I had to practice on the piano for half an hour every day and do the washing up and the dusting, but when I did go out I played ball in Church Street and Castle Street – there was hardly any traffic.
Mary Davies

15 CASTLE STREET

In 1891 John Bidmead, a plasterer, lived here *(Kelly's Directory)*. This is now a record shop, and was previously an antique shop.

I really don't know if this will be classed as a ghost story or not, but it happened to me and was very weird. September 30th 1938 my husband and I married, and it was the same then as now, very difficult to find somewhere to live. We managed to rent two rooms with an elderly lady who was crippled. This was at No. 15, Castle Street. Accommodation was very basic. Although there was an electric light on the outside of the premises neither gas or electricity were available inside. However, to continue, going to bed entailed going along a long corridor to the stairs, which, as soon as I set foot on the first step, I felt that someone was watching me. This feeling stayed with me all of the time we stayed at this house and eventually I just wouldn't go upstairs alone. My husband had just joined the Auxiliary Fire Service and whenever he was called out at night, I got up and waited downstairs until he returned.

One night in particular, when all was very still and quiet, we had retired early to bed and had been in bed perhaps for an hour, when the latch of the bedroom door slowly raised and the door came open about halfway. I know now what it means when your hair stands on end, because I felt my scalp creep, my husband threw his slipper at the door but

no-one came in, I bravely ventured out to the old lady's bedroom and enquired if she was OK. She was furious when I told her what had just happened and told me to return to bed and not talk such nonsense. I felt then that she was aware that something was going on in that house. From then on the dog slept in our bedroom, what help he would have been I can't imagine.

The old lady whom I mentioned before was a cripple and had six cats. In her little back room where she lived was a sofa, table and chair, the table cloth consisted of a sheet of newspaper, on which sat all six cats and for each mouthful she ate, the cats received one each in turn.

I couldn't wait to get away from that spooky house and after two years we were able to move to a little house further down town.

Some years later I met the lady that was now living in the house we had left and I asked her if anything odd went on there. She replied, 'Oh! Only Fred the ghost sometimes, and we don't mind him.' Well, I was jolly glad to leave 'Fred' behind.

Amy Price

THE BLUE BOAR, 16 CASTLE STREET

This was a pub in 1830, and it once had a mounting block. In 1835 John Nixon was the landlord *(Pigot's Directory)*, and in 1891 it was James Webb, who was also a carpenter and builder. In 1926 the landlord was Mrs Sarah Ann Thomas *(Kelly's Directory)*. She was also the midwife. It is a listed building, shown on the 1847 tithe map, with 17th-century origins to the rear. The present landlord is Johnny Golesworthy, one of the family which owns the outfitters' shop near the clock tower.

We went in the Blue Boar one day and in came April Ashley saying loudly: 'You need some bog rolls in the bog.' She had a horrible mangy dog with her and she added: 'I've just been there and it's not very salubrious'. She had eyelashes about a foot long and looked alright as long as you didn't get too close. This was before she inherited Hendre – it was said that his relations weren't too pleased about that. **Eleri Golesworthy**

The Blue Boar was run by Tommy Thomas where Dick Elkington recalls meeting Robert Newton, the film actor and a big drinker.

I've seen the Yanks marching in Hay and they'd go in the Blue Boar, the ones at the back, have a drink and then catch them up. Well, you wouldn't get away with that in the British Army. **Emma Dunn**

17 CASTLE STREET, RUSSELL, BALDWIN AND BRIGHTS

This was a shoe repairer's run by Tommy Alan. **Dick Elkington**

DOLYCOED, 18 CASTLE STREET

This is now Ann Davies and Co. solicitors' offices. In 1875 it was a private school run by Mary Wright. In 1891 Henry Prosser, timber merchant, lived here, and in 1926 Mrs James was the occupant (*Kelly's Directory*).

MORTIMER HOUSE, 19 CASTLE STREET

This is a late Georgian listed building. In 1891 David Morgan lived here. He was the surveyor, collector to the guardians (of the workhouse), registrar of births, marriages and deaths for Hay sub-district and assistant overseer for Hay Rural area, as well as the Inspector of Nuisances.

21 CASTLE STREET

This was a pub called the Golden Lion from 1858-75, though there is a record of a landlord called William Jones in 1835 (*Pigot's Directory*) and in 1891 Charles Gorst was a shopkeeper here (*Kelly's Directory*).

Then there was Brindleys cycle shop, Madigans repairs and petrol pump selling National Benzole (pump at the edge of the pavement). The rest of the places were houses.... **Dick Elkington**

Madigans, where Brin Jenkins is now. Madigans owned the cinema and they also had a cycle shop. **Emma Dunn**

Golden Lion – situated on Mr T.J. Madigan's original cycle shop. **Wisps of Hay**

22 CASTLE STREET

Denny Parry used to be a butcher's. **Emma Dunn**

25 CASTLE STREET

In 1891 James Price Lloyd, plumber and furniture dealer, lived here. In 1926 the occupant was Herbert Batts. He was the relieving and vaccination officer for Hay district, collector to the guardians (of the workhouse), registrar of births, marriages and deaths for Hay sub-district and assistant overseer for Hay Rural area.

The accountants was a house owned by the Batts family who ran an insurance business but just after the war it became a guest house, Spencers. **Dick Elkington**

Where that office is up the steps used to be a tea shop and next to that, only of course they've changed it now because they added that on, there used to be a wallpaper shop, part of the offices now. There were two wallpaper shops in Hay. **Emma Dunn**

SPAR, 26 CASTLE STREET

This is a listed building with 17th-century origins, and was heightened and altered in the 19th century. For a long time it was the Mason's Arms, which was delicensed in 1971, having been licenced for the longest continuous period of all the pubs in Hay. In 1835 Mary Jones was the landlady *(Pigot's Directory)*, and in 1891 the landlord was James Holbrow. Mrs Elkington's mother lived at the Mason's Arms and used to have to scrub the floors of the pub every morning before they opened. In 1987 this was a branch of Fine Fare.

27 CASTLE STREET, GEOFFREY ASPIN'S

This is another listed building, probably dating from the 17th century, but substantially altered. In 1891 David Watkins was a butcher here *(Kelly's Directory)*, and the marble slab is still visible in the front shop window. The sash window originally opened so that customers could be served directly on the street. It was Geoffrey Aspin's bookshop for 21 years, up to his retirement in 1999. There was a slaughter house in Backfold, behind this building.

Where Geoff Aspin was used to be a butcher's. I can remember Reg Parry there because the fellow that had the butcher's where Denny Parry is shot himself in Reg Parry's slaughterhouse. **Emma Dunn**

28 CASTLE STREET, CHRIS GIBBONS' BUTCHERS

This is now Chris Gibbons' butcher's shop. Mr Gibbons is a well-known judge at cattle shows. He has also raised money for Guide Dogs for the Blind by donating £5 worth of meat a week for a year to a prize draw at the British Legion Club. In 1891 Mrs Mary Jane Russell had refreshment rooms here *(Kelly's Directory)*.

The butcher's was a newsagent's run by a Miss Simpson. **Dick Elkington**

I can remember Chris Gibbons being a haberdasher's shop, sold wool and all those sorts of things. Miss Simpkins had it. Then Jones's had it as a sweet shop, and then Grants had it. **Emma Dunn**

29 CASTLE STREET

In 1891 Miss Catherine Chambers and John Chambers (who may be her father or her brother) were bootmakers here *(Kelly's Directory)*.

Then there was another cigarette and sweet shop.
Dick Elkington

30 CASTLE STREET, GREENGROCER'S

In 1926, this was a fishmonger's, owned by Mrs Ann Chambers (some relation to Catherine and John above?) *(Kelly's Directory)*. It is now a greengrocer's, run by Mrs Fields.

Mary Fields has always been a greengrocer's, but they sold pheasants and fish etc. also.
Dick Elkington

Mary Fields has never changed, always been a grocer's. **Emma Dunn**

LION STREET

In 1835, when *Pigot's Directory* was compiled, Lion Street was divided into Red Lion Street and Black Lion Street, and the Half Moon Inn was placed on Old Gravel Lane. Opposite the Wheatsheaf was known as the Pig Market. Most of the people listed below lived or traded on Red Lion Street, though it is impossible to place them precisely.

Mrs Higgins, gentry
William Meredith, blacksmith and gunsmith
Henry Pitt, black (or white) smith
John Price, butcher
John Pritchard, butcher
Richard Bowers, chemist and druggist
John Morgan, currier and leather seller
William Fox, grocer and dealer in sundries

John Morgan, maltster
Richard Williams, nail maker
Edward Kite, stonemason
David Price Owen, surgeon
John Higgins, tailor and draper
William Jones, beer retailer
Thomas Powell, beer retailer

And on Black Lion Street:

Thomas Pugh, tailor

In the Pig Market area there was a turner and chair maker called William Seaborne. In 1858, there was a flannel manufactory near the Black Lion, run by George Jarvis and William Spilman, and including a joiner's shop. This was mentioned in the rates assessment of 1839. In 1858 there were two malt houses in Lion Street, and there was also an iron foundry. Handmade nails were manufactured by several families in the street.

Today, Lion Street is mostly residential from No. 10 to the Wheatsheaf.

I can remember my mother saying that she was talking to someone in Lion Street and Mr Armstrong came along, obviously with two detectives, and my mother said, 'Oh, some poor soul's on today', because he was Clerk of the Court – that was in the year I was born, '23, and they were taking him off. Mother never really had an opinion about it. Webbs lived next door to us and Mr Webb told my mother that they got Mrs Armstrong's body and exhumed it and the only part of the body that had gone bad was on her arm. Well, the arsenic preserved it. She was perfect and her hair was still growing – her hair was long. The Webbs were undertakers. **Emma Dunn**

PROMINENT BUILDINGS ON LION STREET

ST JOHN'S CHAPEL

Before the Reformation, this was a chantry chapel and chapel for the Guild of Tradesmen, and is said to have been founded in 1254. It also served as the chapel to the castle. It was dissolved as a chantry in 1547 by Edward VI and transferred to the Vaughan family in 1567. When Leland visited Hay during his tour of the country in 1568, he heard mass here. The priest was paid with the interest on capital loaned out at 20% interest, bringing in an income of £3.3s.3d a year. As well as saying masses for the dead the priest here held 'morrow masses', services held at dawn so that people on their way to work could worship. The first recorded name of a priest at St John's is in 1558, when William Hyde was paid 4/- for saying mass once a year, though the name of the person commemorated is not recorded. The boundary of the parish of St John's was the town wall, and the parish church of Hay, St Mary's, is outside the wall.

In 1684, the chapel building was being used as a school, as it is mentioned as such in Dineley's account of the progress of the first Duke of Beaufort through Wales as Lord President of the Council of Wales and Lord Warden of the Marches. His illustration shows a clear line of sight between St John's and the Black Swan inn on Broad Street.

When John Wesley visited Hay in 1774, he preached 'within the walls of the old church' and a footnote adds that the older church of St John's fell down in 1700 and was never restored. The court rolls for 1774 and 1775 record the complaint: 'We present a great quantity of stone, being fell from the ruings of St John's church in this Borough as a great nuisance and ought to be from thence removed'. However, under the name Church Evan, it appears to have still been used for services, according to the records of St Mary's, where repairs to the door and bell are mentioned until 1811. The bell is still being used today, and was mounted in the present belfry in 1934, when the church was rebuilt. It bears the inscription 'Ifan. Edward Wellington. 1718'.

In 1810, the building was converted into a lockup by Mr Henry Wellington, according to the testimony of David Jones, the oldest inhabitant of Hay at the time, who referred to Henry Wellington as 'a kind of king in Hay and did exactly as he liked'. It continued to be a lockup until 1875, when it was pronounced insanitary, and the police station was built.

After this, the building was used as a butcher's, saddler's and barber's shop and a temporary bank and school, as well as the Fire Station for a time, until it was bought by Mary Louisa Dawson in 1930 and rebuilt as a church in 1934.

The town pound for stray animals was through a small door, now walled up, on the left-hand side of the one leading to St John's Rooms.

St John's used to be a bank. I can remember it as a bank but somebody told me that before that it was a butcher's shop. As a bank I remember somebody hanging themselves in there, a young man of the staff and Katy Evans used to clean there. Katy Evans is Mary Fields' mother. She used to do Barclay's bank as well. She did it for donkey's years. She was quite old, I think in her 80s, when she gave up. She found the fellow hanging when she went in in the morning. I would say that was in the 1930s. **Emma Dunn**

HAY PARISH HALL

In 1890 Rev Bevan set up the Infants School in the new parish hall, and Mary Jane Barrett was the first mistress. In 1926, Mrs C.E. (Kate) Morris was the mistress *(Kelly's Directory)*. There was provision for 75 children and the average attendance was 60.

BEECH HOUSE

The exact location of this house is unknown, but it was the Drover's Arms in 1902.

THE HALF MOON

This is a listed building, and is known to have been a pub from 1830 to 1970. In a plan of a sale of property in 1861, this part of Lion Street was named Half Moon Street. It had a mounting block at one time, and is of 18th-century origin. In 1835 the landlord was William Jones, and the street was called Old Gravel Lane *(Pigot's Directory)*. In 1891 the landlady was Mrs Martha Jones, and in1926 the publican was Mrs Margaret Price *(Kelly's Directory)*.

Haydn Pugh had his print shop here before he moved to the shop on Brecon Road which is now Doll's House Fun. The interior has also been altered as office accommodation.

The Half Moon was one of the oldest pubs in the town. That's the pink building right opposite the Parish Hall. There were over 30 pubs in Hay at that time. **Rex Jones**

The Half Moon pub was, my husband said, the best pub in Hay. Arthur Lewis was the landlord; his wife was called Myra. If you had any problems at all he would always have a bit of advice. **Eleri Golesworthy**

1 LION STREET

Now the oriental carpet shop, this is another listed building, dating from the late 18th century. In 1987, when the listing was taking place, it was the Ich Dien Dairy Ice Cream shop.

2 LION STREET

Now Hay Wholefoods, the building is listed as part of a group that includes No. 1 and No. 3. It has 18th-century origins with 19th-century alterations.

The health food shop was Meadow Dairy – a grocery shop again. **Emma Dunn**

It was from the window of the first floor flat that a police marksman kept watch on the dentist's opposite during the Hay siege (see 43 Lion Street).

3 LION STREET

Now Dai & Chris Davies' newsagents, and listed as above.

Where the paper shop is, that used to be a shoe shop, Tommy Griffiths. **Emma Dunn**

I was living at that time in Lion Street where Derek Addyman has the bookshop now and we went to sleep that night. Living opposite, in the paper shop, was a Mr Tom Griffiths, a shoemaker, and about 4.00 in the morning I heard a noise and got up and I disturbed my brother, who got up as well. We looked through the window and were firmly of the opinion that someone was breaking into Mr Griffiths'. We made our way downstairs – my father heard us and came after us, and he said, 'You hang on a minute until I'm ready' so we went out and there was Dr Powell, one of our local doctors who lived at what's Kilvert's now, and the Steward of the [Conservative] Club was trying to open Mr Griffiths' door. It was between 3.00 and 4.00 in the morning; the Club had been opened that night and he'd had too much to drink and couldn't get the key in the lock. So, there were no burglars but just three men who'd been celebrating. **Reg Lewis**

4 LION STREET

Now the AonY bookshop, and listed with the group of buildings on this side of the street.

5 LION STREET

Now the Murder and Mayhem bookshop, owned by Derek and Ann Addyman, whose main shop, Addyman's, is opposite.

Opposite Addymans I can remember it being a fish shop and I can remember it being a hairdresser's. **Emma Dunn**

There was a glass engraver where Murder and Mayhem is now, run by a man who used to be a jockey. **Eleri Golesworthy**

The ex-jockey was called David, and he used to lead children on pony treks. Once he was well up into the Black Mountains when they stopped for a rest, and one of the kids said: 'Where's the nearest shop?' He wanted to buy sweets. So, all seriousness, David sent him off into the bushes. When he came back, he said 'I can't find it.' 'Oh,' said David, 'It must be closed. **Lesley Arrowsmith**

6 LION STREET

Horsewise used to be a gentleman's outfitters, Pugh's. They were quite up market but also his father had where the Oxfam is now. **Emma Dunn**

[Mr Pugh] used to keep a drapers' shop on the corner where Horsewise is now; he and his son Trevor Pugh. **Rex Jones**

Trevor Pugh had an outfitter's where Horsewise is now, and he used to stand in the shop doorway with his arms folded all day. **Eleri Golesworthy**

8 LION STREET

In 1882, Mr John Edwin Hope lived here. He had a son in Australia to whom he wrote with news of Hay.

10 LION STREET

In 1926 Richard Evans, bootmaker, lived here *(Kelly's Directory)*. It is now a private house.

13 LION STREET

It is now a private house.

Mrs Eves boiled toffee for generations of schoolchildren. **Wisps of Hay**

15 LION STREET

Now Rainbow pre-school Nursery.

19 LION STREET

The building is now home to Lion Street Fine Arts and Antiques, owned by Charles and Sylvia Spencer.

Then there's the Black Lion and opposite it where there's an antique shop now there was Bill Powell the butcher. He used to do a round with a van.
Rex Jones

20 LION STREET

Part of this building was, for a short time, the premises of specialist bookstore Rare Comics. It is now a B&B.

My grandfather was the undertaker in the town. The place where Humphrey Webb was where Underhill's garage is now. They had a garage and an undertaker's business there and they stored a lot of stuff at the bottom of Oxford Road. It's a hairdresser's

now. They had a place at the bottom of Bear Street here, which is a flat behind the antique shop. The shop was a butcher's for many years until Mr Keylock died and then it's been an antique shop since. Humphrey Webb lived right opposite where we're sitting now in Bear Street.

My mother was one of 13 children. **Reg Lewis**

The Garage where Phillip Gittins is now used to belong to H.C. Webb & Sons. They ran a garage with a taxi service but he was also the local undertaker. They used to make the coffins where the workshop is now and then they used to store the coffin boards where the hairdresser's is over the road now in a double-doored garage. It was packed out. The coffins were all handmade. A man called Roley Probert who lived at Cusop made them. They were wonderful creations, works of art then. They used to do a lot of hospital runs and school runs and things like that.

Then La Fosse guest house…. There was an old boy named Frank Parry used to live up at Cusop and one of his jaunts on a Saturday night was to go and have three or four pints and then go home, and his one port of call was this little red brick urinal opposite the television shop. On several occasions after it was demolished Frank Parry would come down, quite an elderly gentleman by then, he'd come all the way along, go up onto the bank, walk round as if he was going into the urinal, have a Jimmy Riddle on the bank and then carry on home.
Rex Jones

21 LION STREET

Where Jill Williams' brother works, he does engines, well, that used to be the carpenter shop for the school. Hay School had their own carpentry shop.
Emma Dunn

25 LION STREET, THE DRILL HALL

This is a late 19th-century building, the original title being the Volunteers' Institute and Drill Hall as well as being the headquarters of the D Company and H (Mounted Infantry) Company of the 1st Breconshire Volunteer Battalion South Wales Borderers (it housed concerts and a working men's club with reading and coffee rooms).

In the 1890s Mr Clifford King, who became an actor in Lillie Langtry's company, returned to Hay and gave recitals in the Drill Hall for various charities. In his publicity, he was called 'the noted Shakespearean actor'.

During this decade, detachments of the Royal Artillery came every year to camp about 2 miles from the town, from 1st June to mid-August, and trained daily, except Thursdays, on the Black Mountains.

In 1891, the Drill Hall was the seat of the County Court, held every alternate month. The commander of the Drill Hall volunteers was Capt. Edmund Hall Cheese, the solicitor from Broad Street who was also clerk to the magistrates. The drill instructor was Sgt. George Monoghan. The captain of the Mounted Infantry, which seems to have been a separate body of men, was Capt. Penry Lloyd, and their drill instructor was Sgt. William Griffith. The registrar and high bailiff of the County Court was George Henry Page *(Kelly's Directory)*.

In the period following the First World War, the building was used for dances, and Mr Armstrong the solicitor was reputed to have been a fine dancer. The building is now Edward Foreman's Book Warehouse, one of the biggest bookshops in Hay. Mr Foreman came to Hay to work for Richard Booth, having originally worked in the family printing business in Surrey. Sport Fish were the previous occupants.

For lack of information I cannot properly close the story of the proposed Working Men's Club, headquarters of which were at the Drill Hall. There, a Committee, formed in the early part of 1878, came to the conclusion a favourable opportunity for the project 'offered itself' and 'the time was right'. Stated objects – as expounded in Minutes were, 'to supply a need where men can meet for social purposes and spend their evenings in such ways as may suit their own tastes, i.e. in talking, reading, smoking, playing games, etc.' Very nice – no 'telly', no women! No Wallop!

The Committee further ordained 'that members of the Club should be able to obtain NON-INTOXICATING refreshments on their own premises – and this, accordingly forms part of the scheme'.

(Snag: Pubs – Black Lion, Drovers Arms, Travellers' Trap, New Inn, Bear and Bell – were then right atop the Volunteers' Drill Hall). I have been unable to check on the suggestion that on Club night, the opening chorus was, 'Yield not to Temptation'.

Then, when the Working Men's Club was established on November 8th, 1878 – there were elected to the Permanent Committee – and it was ever thus in those days - a selection of local big-wigs, who by no stretch of the imagination would ever plead guilty to belonging to the 'Working Class', or even associating with it, save in a condescending way. Here's a selection – Archdeacon W.L. Bevan, Hay Castle, and, of course, Vicar of St Mary's; Mr Trumper (a lawyer?), Brook House; Mr J.L. Davies (Chemist, and, purveyor, later, of considerable quantities of arsenic to Justices' Clerk and poisoner, Major Armstrong); Mr Jones, schoolmaster, Belmont House and Dr C.S. Clouston. BUT – also co-opted were these: John Bevan, Lion Street; W.P. Bird, Bear St; W. Burchell, Garibaldi Terrace; David Davies, Heol-y-dwr; James Foxley, Lion Street; Tho. Hinksman, Heol-y-dwr; Alexander Lane, Gas-works; R. Owen, Black Lion Green; Phillip Pembridge, Brook St; Charles Roberts, Belmont Rd; James Pugh, Lion St; Amos Morgan, Heol-y-dwr; Tom Parry, Castle St.

That would seem to give the 'working class' element a nice majority, but the guiding fingers of the Permanent Committee would be well and truly spread in the Club pie.

Thus the Archdeacon at the opening, expressed his hope 'that the Club might be conducive to the happiness of the working men of Hay and the general welfare of the District.' And – so states St Mary's Magazine, which was the Archdeacon's Trumpet – 'He brought an interesting address to an end by telling 'the working men that the

Management of the institution was now in GREAT PART IN THEIR HANDS.'
St. Mary's Church Magazine

Mrs Maddy has a programme for 'A Midsummer Night's Dream' at the Drill Hall, when lots of local people were fairies and elves.

Where the bookshop and warehouse is now, used to be the Drill Hall where they ran the local Home Guard and the shooting range up on the first floor and the dance hall was up there. That was a famous dance floor, they used to have weekly dances there and where the end of it that's been converted to a house, was the actual Army TA offices and Home Guard offices and my father worked there for donkeys' years. **Rex Jones**

During the war Nancy and I could go out for half a crown. That was twenty fags, shandy and a shilling to go in the dance. **Emma Dunn**

Where the TV video shop is now was a family grocer's, Leonard Stephens and he had a bakehouse behind – they still bake in that bakehouse, that's the original one and after it was taken over by the man that used to do the delivery round for him. He bought the business off Mr Stephens – Mr Alfie Jones who still lives at Cusop. He's in his 90s now. **Rex Jones**

26 Lion Street, The Famous Old Black Lion

A listed building which is said to have 13th-century origins, it stands beside the position of the former Lion Gate. The present structure is mainly 17th century and the frontage was brought forward in the 18th century. There are also some modern additions.

Allen and I were taken down to the cellar by John Collins, the landlord at the time, to see the cobbled floor surface which he believed to be medieval, and the chances of this being true are good.
Lesley Arrowsmith

The interior retains considerable 17th-century detail, including exposed beams in the bar and some 17th-century panelling upstairs. There is also Georgian panelling. The most interesting room is the Cromwell Room formed out of the flooring of an open roof hall – it retains the half loft/gallery with a modern balustrade.

In 1835 John Allen was the landlord, and this part of the street is recorded as New Street *(Pigot's Directory)*. In 1891 John Probert was the landlord, and in 1926 it was James Williams *(Kelly's Directory)*. In the 19th century it was the home of the Black Lion Friendly Society, which saved money for respectable burials, and sickness and accident insurance. Rev Richard Lloyd's tomb was provided by the society in 1797.

In 1971, the pub wasn't expected to have its license renewed. At this time, most of the features mentioned above were obscured, with the décor being formica tables and fluorescent lighting. When John and Joan Collins were renovating the bar, they wanted to open up the inglenook fireplace which they knew to exist, opposite the door to the bar, which now has a large settle in front of it. When they tried, though, they found that some sort of supporting bar had been inserted, and they had to reseal it.

In 1987, when the details were taken for listing the building, part of the pub was an antique shop.

The Black Lion was the worst pub for rowdiness in Hay – my grandfather lived in a cottage at the back of Hendre and said the noise was awful. Even he didn't dare go down there. He said that in Hay you had to either be a drunkard or a religious fanatic, there was nothing else to do. **Vera Fairfax**

HAY BINDERS

This workshop is in an un-numbered building next to No. 27.

At the end of Lion Street immediately facing you was the old Police Station, which is now a guest house and the next building to that was a blacksmith's farrier shop for years. Mr Ward was the blacksmith. You could smell the burning horses' feet and I used to watch them many a day. Then there was a big house where we used to get doughnuts after school. One day I went to get one but didn't have any money. You used to put the money in a drawer and I said I'd put it in, but he opened the drawer and there wasn't any money there so I got told off.
Rex Jones

THE OLD POLICE STATION

The Police Station used to be next to Wards, Roy Jones now, and they had cells and all that. Mr Armstrong was locked up there.

There were some people come to Hay, travellers, you know. They used to call the lane that runs up past our place Gipsy Castle Lane, and all the gipsies used to park up there. The police found they'd been stealing money from banks and they had to go to a place like Hay and get caught! They found all the money stuffed into spare tyres on the wagons and I can remember the police coming to my mum's, because my mum used to have a very big plait and they asked if she would she go on an identification parade, and I kept saying 'Don't you go, mum, because they might pick you'. They held up banks from Evesham down and they got to Hay and got caught. A policeman called Mr Richards got them. We were living at 14 Bear Street so I must have been about twelve to realise what identification was. They wanted my mum to put her plait round her head like this woman had it and my mother went to the police station and she said they'd opened a feather bed where they'd found money, because my mother said, 'What? Are they going to tar and feather them?'

[After the police station closed] where they do Bed and Breakfast now – if any inspectors had gone in that shop they'd have closed it down. I mean, when he used to sell something he had a slit in the counter and he dropped the money in that way – never opened the drawer unless he had to get change. Made his own bread and he made wonderful, wonderful hot cross buns. People used to queue there for hot cross buns. **Emma Dunn**

34 LION STREET

My great grandfather lived in 34 Lion Street in 1880-90. He worked on building the railway between Brecon and Hay and my grandfather was a mason who built the railway bridges. My grandfather's name was Evan Lloyd. **Vera Fairfax**

35 LION STREET, THE CONSERVATIVE CLUB

We played badminton and tennis on a private court at the side of what is now the Conservative Club, where there was a bowling green as well that belonged to a Mr Pugh. A lady who lived near Clyro let us use her tennis court if we cleared it up. **Tony Pugh**

Mrs Maddy used to go to dancing classes at what was the Liberal Club, and there were tennis courts and a flourishing tennis club. Chancery Court used to be a garden. A part of it belonged to Brook House and there were tennis courts at the back there and the garden went right through to Heol-y-dwr. **Emma Dunn**

Where that new housing block is next to the Conservative Club, used to be the Bowling Green and Tennis Courts run by Mr Pugh. He used to keep a draper's shop on the corner where Horsewise is now; he and his son Trevor Pugh. The house that went with the tennis courts and bowling green was the guest house in Brook Street, Brookfield House. The Farmers Co-op bought it up and put a big seed drying building there that's disappeared now. When you came further along the street you got the Conservative Club, the old Constitutional Club, and then on the left were small cottages. Some have been done up by Terry Salter over the years. **Rex Jones**

The new club opened in 1937. The old Conservative Club was where the British Legion Club is now.
Reg Lewis

37 LION STREET

This is a listed building, shown on the 1847 tithe map. For a short time it was Marijana Dworski's East European bookshop, and now houses an antique shop.

My grandfather was a mason and lived in Hay, near the present community centre. He was a terrible boozer. The Salvation Army used to have open meetings when the band played and then they marched down to the Hall on the first floor of the building next to the Wheatsheaf. One night he and a group of other 'yobbos' decided to break up the meeting. They followed the band down to the Hall

Top: Evan Lloyd, stonemason of Glasbury, Vera Fairfax's great-grandfather, born 1812, died 1881, with his wife (middle) (originally from Cwmbach) and, of their eleven children – daughter, Bessie and son, Evan Lloyd II, also stonemason of Glasbury, born 1857, died 1952

and he went in, prepared to heckle. He came face to face with the woman who was to become my grandmother, who was very beautiful. He took one look at her and never touched another drop for the rest of his life! **Vera Fairfax**

Mrs Lilwall played the squeeze box at meetings. **Wisps of Hay**

Further along from the Wheatsheaf was the old Salvation Army Hall, right opposite St. John's. **Rex Jones**

They had a Hall up top and you used to go there, you know, for services. The antique shop [now Marina's antique shop] used to be a solicitors. **Emma Dunn**

38 Lion Street, The Wheatsheaf

This pub has been licensed since 1830. It is a late 17th-century building with 19th-century alterations. The interior is said to be largely altered, but retains a rubble fireplace with timber lintel on the ground floor. In 1835 Hannah Parry was the landlady and the street was known as the Pig Market *(Pigot's Directory)*. The pig market was set up outside St. John's Chapel, opposite, and a ring in the wall of the chapel still remains where the hurdles for the pig pens were fastened. Sir Joseph Bailey, Lord of the Manor and thus in charge of the market, was petitioned to pave the area during the 19th century because of the mess left by the pigs.

A friend of Richard Booth's, April Ashley, used to say things about Hay that I didn't go much on. She stood outside by the town clock and there was a picture of her in the paper and it said April Ashley says: 'If I can change, why can't Hay?' I told her I didn't go much on it and we had a real up and downer. She told me to go away in no uncertain terms in the Wheatsheaf one night because I was both the Borough Councillor in Brecon and the County Councillor in Llandrindod Wells, yet when she comes to Hay she always calls to see how I am. 'Oh, darling Rex', she'd say.

She was a character and you couldn't help but like her. You had to meet her to believe her. You couldn't believe that she wasn't a woman. She used to buy a lot of ex-theatrical things and was done up to the nines. One night April was sat at the bar in the Wheatsheaf on a stool and she had this gorgeous cream trouser suit on – she was as brown as a berry — and her hair was in a light ginger bob; her nails were absolutely perfect and her toe-nails were painted. How could a bloody man look like that? I said I want the tablets that April Ashley's on. **Mr & Mrs Rex Jones**

39 Lion Street

This is now Addyman's bookshop, where **Ann Brichto** has found old receipts in the shop from the time of Morgans.

In 1891, Thomas Cyrus Morgan, manure agent and aerated water manufacturer, lived here *(Kelly's Directory)*. Between 1983-86 this was the premises of the Children's Bookshop and Clock Shop, owned by Bob and Judith Gardner. It has also been a restaurant and something to do with the hardware shop on High Town. It is a listed building, shown on the 1847 tithe map.

I can remember Addyman's being a corn merchants. They used to do those bottles of pop with a marble in them. That's why we called him Tom Pop — his real name was Tom Price. He used to make the pop there, do wholesale, and you could buy a bottle there too. Of course, then we used to smash the bottle to get the marble out. **Emma Dunn**

40 LION STREET

In 1891, Richard Evans, bootmaker, lived here. It was also the premises for the agent of the Singer Manufacturing Company sewing machine manufacturers, Frederick Larcombe *(Kelly's Directory)*. In 1891, there were six tailors and four dressmakers in Hay, as well as two milliners and several draper's, so there was plenty of call for the services of the Singer manufacturers. There were also two clothing warehouses and outfitters, but many Hay people wore clothes that had been individually made for them. This is now Hay Design & Print and the Hay Video shop.

Where the video shop is was a shoe repair shop. **Emma Dunn**

The video shop was an antique shop, run by Annie and a friend. **Eleri Golesworthy**

41 LION STREET, THE RED LION

This is a listed building, at the east end of a row of gable ended frontages midway along the street. It is said to have been a Recabite Hall *(see appendix)* and was formerly the Red Lion Inn. The building's core is a 17th-century, timber-framed construction with 19th-century alterations, which include the shop front. It is now John and June Jones's import gift shop and vegetable/fruit shop.

At the back of the yard was a shed which was once a licensed meeting place for Quakers. As a pub, it was licensed before 1776, possibly up to 1903. In 1835 the landlord was William Boore when the street was called Red Lion Street *(Pigot's Directory)*. In 1891 James Price, cabinet maker and builder, lived here, and in 1926 it was D. Evans, groce's. It has been a grocer's ever since, which makes it one of the shops with the longest single use in Hay. A small part of the shop was split off to provide premises for Karen Smart's Pine Cellar, which later moved to Backfold, and was replaced by Meridian Art Gallery.

My father had a greengrocer's and I ran it with him and after he died. It had been a pub – the Red Lion, and he rented a room, then eventually bought the pub out and had a greengrocer's. One of the great things I remember as a child was the May Fair – a Red Letter Day. I was involved in a way because the shop, and all the others along the street, used to put their goods out on trestles, outside the shops, in the road. I would say that Lion Street was a very happy street. There were lots of practical jokes played – my father was a one for that. He and a neighbour, Mr Prosser, a shoemaker, would hatch up a practical joke to play on another Mr Pugh who ran an outfitter's shop. You could tell the time by when certain people came into the shop in those days. **Tony Pugh**

The room above where John and June's fruit shop is used to be the Hall for the Ancient Order of Foresters. They had a branch there for years, and the Royal Antediluvian Order of Buffaloes – they both had societies here. I think they're defunct now but they were both flourishing in my lifetime. **Rex Jones**

Pughs have always been there, about 90 years, and his father and mother used to sell fish, fresh fish, so they didn't have any windows on that one side, it was all open. Where they've got that little shop next to John's, that was the living quarters of Pughs. Their shop didn't go back as far as it does now because they lived over the top. Everybody lived over their shops. **Emma Dunn**

Caption: T.J .Pugh's, 41 Lion Street

'Kipper' Pugh at the greengrocer's was a terrible tease. **Eleri Golesworthy**

He said there's been a grocer's there since 1870-something and he was very upset it's going to be a craft shop. **Derek Addyman**

42 LION STREET

Next door where the Chinese restaurant is, there was Evans the Stores. Now Evans was later owned by Budgets of Bristol and that's where I come into it. Evans the Stores were a family firm in Talgarth and they had a shop in Talgarth, one in Glasbury and one in Hay. Budget's of Bristol took them over. I worked for Budget's for a while and used to be in Talgarth, Glasbury and I knew the fellows at the London Central Meat Company as well. I used to drive all round for the firm – Painscastle, Newchurch, Llandeilo, I used to go with a man from Talgarth, so he was the driver, not me. My brother had this shop in Hay and he let the thing go west. I was in school in Brecon and my father brought me home from the school to look after the shop and I looked after it. A friend of mine, who was a Like, a brother to Geoff Like who had the garage, an uncle to Michael Like, he said he worked for Budget's of Bristol and said 'Why don't you come and work for Budget's and sell the shop to them?' I said they wouldn't buy it but he said they would, so a fellow came along to see it and offered my father far more than it was worth. I thought, there's a catch here somewhere, and as he finished he said, 'Look, there's only one thing. If you sell us the shop, your son has got to work for us for four years. At the end of four years he can do what he likes'. My father said, 'Well, I can't tell you to do that,' and I said, 'Well, you've condemned me to a lifetime of it now, I'm never going to get out of it or else you're just going to shut it and lose everything,' and I said I'd do it. I signed this contract and that's how I went to work for them. Then of course the war started and the old solicitor that was here then where Mr Beale's office is now, came along and he said he wanted to see me in his office. In those days you said 'Yes, sir, I'll be down.' He said he'd looked through my contract and the war had started and if I joined the army they had no claim on me. I had a friend who was a footman for a Professor Merton and he'd been at Winforton Court and I told him about it. 'D'you know,' he said, 'I'm standing in the corner, down at Winforton Court, saying yes or no, sir, three bags full, sir, and I'm fed up with it.' I said 'So am I'.

That night we'd both had a drink, to be honest, and my mother said 'You can't ride that home, you've been drinking,' and normally he didn't drink. It was only a pushbike, mind. Anyway, he came to my bedroom and the following morning we got up early and left a note on the table and went off and joined the RAF. I never went back to the shop. The first time I was on leave I met old Trumpery the solicitor again and he asked how I was getting on. I said 'Fine, thanks,' and he said, 'You made a bloody mistake. You joined that Brylcream lot instead of joining the army'. Of course, he'd been a major in the army, but the old boy was very good to me, to be fair. **Reg Lewis**

43 LION STREET

The dentist's surgery until late 1999, and the scene of the Hay siege in December, 1993. Edward Mark Williams, 28, attempted to murder his foster mother, Mrs Sylvia Taylor, in Llangammarch Wells, and fled to Hay, where he tried to sell her car. The buyer, Kevin Nichols of Little Fford Fawr, was suspicious of him and drove him to the Nat West bank in Hay, while his father called the police. He attempted to cash a cheque there.

Williams was on licence from prison, where he was serving a sentence for being involved in an armed robbery six years earlier. PC Ken Murray confronted Williams in the bank to be held at gunpoint, and forced to hand over his police radio and keys. However, he was able to escape as they walked through Hay and raised the alarm. Williams then went into the chemist's and held Mr Pattison at gunpoint, taking him to the CAB office and the Kilvert Hotel before going into the dentist's. The dentist, Christopher Edge, also escaped. Ten hostages were taken upstairs; dentist Nigel Huw Williams, dental receptionist Pauline Margaret Williams, dental nurses Wendy Rees and Valerie Anne Hamer, hygienist Joan Edith Davies and patients William Bruce Hosie, Rosalind Mary Coles the vet, and Jannet Izena Gwynne. Several children were booked in for that afternoon, but fortunately had not arrived.

Armed police surrounded the area and cordoned off the street. At 5.15pm, three women were rescued from Marches Gallery, opposite the dentist's. By 6pm there were fifty armed police officers in Hay. At 6.30pm, eleven portions of fish and chips were delivered to the hostages by means of a knotted sheet let down from the window. The school was opened as a centre for the SAS and police. The Christmas lights remained on all night instead of being switched off at 11pm as normal, so that Williams wouldn't be alarmed into thinking the police were about to storm the building. The siege went on through the night, and at 5am, Williams dozed off. One woman hostage then attacked him with an umbrella and Joan Davies, the hygienist, wrestled a gun from him. She said later that she was convinced that the guns were imitation, which proved to be the case. The siege was over. The police later praised the courage and level-headedness of the hostages.

Down at the chip shop on Broad Street, the Radcliffes were kept busy all night providing toast and other snacks to the film crews who set up all round the clock tower.

Mark Williams was later sentenced to four life sentences.

The BBC later re-enacted the siege for the programme 'In Extreme Danger', for which local shops dressed their windows for Christmas several months ahead of time.

The next place was a butcher's shop where the dentist has been. That's where you see the green tiles on the outside because it was the London Central Meat Company. All they sold was lamb and it was New Zealand imported lamb. They were there for many years. **Reg Lewis**

Going up from Richard Booth's, that used to be a New Zealand lamb shop and all they sold was New Zealand lamb, and it used to be a hairdresser's. **Emma Dunn**

44 LION STREET

This is The Limited, which is now Richard Booth's bookshop. In 1891 Charles Hastings was recorded in *Kelly's Directory* as being a watchmaker here, though this is unlikely, as the building is huge, and was probably part of Robert Williams and Sons agricultural showrooms at the time, as they built it in 1886. There is a shield held by a lion at the gable, inscribed 'R.W.&S. 1886'. However, it may already have been part of a complex of buildings including the Granary on Broad Street. At the end of the First World War, a Grand Ball was held in the upper floor of the showroom to celebrate. The building was lit with electricity, with coloured fairy lights and a temporary chandelier, thanks to Mr Lilwall, who supplied the first electric power in Hay. His power station was in Heol-y-dwr.

Major Booth drove one of the first cars in Hay, a clattering, chain driven, perambulating summer house, daily from his home in Cusop into Hay.
Wisps of Hay

This attractive, largely wooden building was built as the Agricultural Hall for Robert Williams and Son, general dealers in agricultural supplies and implements. The lion's head above relates to the street's name while the picture tiles on the frontage are of rural and farming designs. Formerly the frontage was open for the display of the larger farming machines manufactured by the firm. As the largest covered accommodation in Hay the upper floor of the building was used for many public functions, banquets or balls being held here to celebrate Queen Victoria's Jubilee and Victory in 1918. When Robert Williams became a Limited Company it was the only local business in the town with such status and rapidly became known as 'The Limited', a name which the building has retained ever since. **Walking Round Hay**

The Limited hardware used to be where Andy Cooke is – at the corner of the Pavement. Where Richard is they used to sell implements for the farms and furniture, second hand furniture. It all belonged to the Limited because it used to have the yard where the Co-op is now (in Newport Street) as a sawmills. My father used to work at the sawmills for years and years. Someone once came – and you know how they take chips off wood – well someone came to buy some of that off them and he said to my father, 'What am I supposed to do with them?' and my father said, 'Bag'em'. My father got called Bag'em for the rest of his life. **Emma Dunn**

Annie's shop (Marches Gallery) was part of the Limited and sold china. They had the most wonderful glass and china in The Limited. **Eleri Golesworthy**

45 LION STREET

In 1891 Thomas Jones the tailor lived here and it was also the premises of George Perry Price the auctioneer *(Kelly's Directory)*. It is now divided into the haberdasher's and the flower shop.

Then round the corner was a Mrs Williams who had a café and then Miss Hastings the jeweller and you came to where the flower shop is.... **Reg Lewis**

June's and the flower shop were one shop with a huge window and Rita Like sold furniture there. There was a gardening shop along there. **Eleri Golesworthy**

46 LION STREET

This is now Acedia booksearch and bookshop, and is part of the Golesworthy's range of buildings. It forms part of a group of listed buildings, and is early 19th century in date, though it is thought to have 18th-century timber-framed origins. In 1987, it was the premises of Golden Pioneer Travel.

Mrs Lewis had a jewellery shop in Lion Street at the end of Golesworthy's. **Eleri Golesworthy**

One jeweller's shop was next to Golesworthys, Hastings, quite a small shop. If you bought a wedding ring you had a box of spoons with it. My wedding ring came from Hastings and I had a little box of teaspoons with it, that they used to give you. **Emma Dunn**

47 LION STREET

This is a listed building, and the premises of Golesworthy's outfitters. In 1891 it was home to C.J. Curtis and Co. clothing and boot warehouse, and was later taken over by its rivals. One of the Golesworthy family remembers playing with 1920s shoes from the store room as a child in the 1970s.

I first visited Hay just after Christmas 1950 to stay with my future husband's parents. Just before Christmas I was rushed into hospital with peritonitis and I couldn't go all the way to North Wales (I was living in Cheltenham) so I came on the bus to Hay. My husband lived with his parents at 47 Lion Street behind the shop. It was a shock to me as they didn't talk at mealtimes, and after eating his father would retreat behind a book and his mother would knit. I went to the library once, which was then in what are the council offices now; there was a french window into the library where there is a bow window now, but they said to me, 'there isn't a book here that your father-in-law hasn't read'. Anyway, I kept talking when I first visited and my father-in-law to be lowered his book and said 'Doesn't that girl ever stop talking?' to which his wife replied, 'Well, I expect she comes from a family that talks rather more than we do!'.

The shop was a bit smaller in those days, didn't have the bit next door that belonged to Jones's In the passageway was a boiler that looked like an ancient monument. Roger and Anna lived next door in what is now the bar of the Granary, with the leaded light windows. Jones's sold boots and shoes.

My in-laws had a bridge night every Thursday for eight people. Although rationing was still on my mother-in-law made some lovely cakes for it, and the people who always came were Beryl Jones, a teacher, Sophie Morgan, the District Nurse, Mrs Ralph Jones (of the shop), Margaret Williams, head of the Infants School, Mrs Birch (Nigel's mother), and Miss Browning, who was a hairdresser.

My husband grew up in Hay and all his friends had nicknames – Slim, Shirty, Goosy, Clutterweb, Chicken, Elkie, Boney and Sponge Cake. My husband was called Guzzy.

There were a lot of horses and carts about in those days; you couldn't always get petrol. Mr Roderick had a farm and delivered milk on a horse and cart, bringing cream on Sunday mornings. Mr Roderick used to have a churn full of milk and a dipper. I always went to talk with him in Welsh. I went to see him just before he died at Dorstone because Eleri Hopkins was running a programme for S4C and asked for five Welsh speakers to talk about Hay. He was nearly 90 then and said, 'If only they'd asked me 20 years ago'. I couldn't get five people willing and able to speak Welsh.

[April Ashley] had a heart attack and collapsed in my father-in-law's doorway and when the ambulance men came they said, 'Which ward are we going to put her in?' **Eleri Golesworthy**

BEAR STREET

The Bear (T. Price), The New Inn (A. Powell).
Wisps of Hay

There was a 'Common Lodging House' in Heol y Dwr but in about 1905 a Mr Greenaway built a 'model' lodging house in Bear Street (Hendre) for workers and charged a penny or two more a night. It had a lovely white front doorway with stained glass. My grandfather told him, 'It's no good putting that in for the type of men you're going to have to stay there'.

'Nothing is too good for my boys,' said Mr Greenaway but on the very first Saturday night a bottle went through it and smashed it. **Vera Fairfax**

THE BULL RING

The Bell (T. Pugh). **Wisps of Hay**

The fire station was right on the corner. I remember the fire station being there and opposite – you know that rather nice house? There was a blacksmith there between the house and the Baptist Chapel, Turners the blacksmith. There used to be two blacksmiths in Hay. **Emma Dunn**

BULL RING ANTIQUES

Mac Maddy's family had a grocer's shop here. It was started by his great grandfather 150 years ago and was called Kennedys at first, later altered to Maddys. They had a bakehouse where the British Legion Club is now and made all their own bread and cakes, the baker being a Mr Pitt, (Lily Pitt's grandfather, father and brother all carried on the tradition) and their cakes were famous. Mr Maddy retired 20 years ago, letting it to a grocer, Mr. Dimbylow, but they asked permission ten years ago to change it to an antique shop.

Maddys the grocer's was wonderful, like Harrods. **Eleri Golesworthy**

The lady who ran the shop was called Delphine, and they decided to stop trading as grocers when Lo-Cost opened on the edge of town. **Lesley Arrowsmith**

There were three people working in the bakery and eight in the shop, doing their deliveries first of all by horse and cart and later with a van. The shop used to supply the old Workhouse and I can remember a notice above the mantelpiece which read: 'The inmates are not to be served fresh Wye salmon more than 2 (or 3 - I can't remember the exact words) times a week'. The workhouse was run by Brecon Council and housed tramps. There was one called Jim who used to go around town with a handcart selling firewood, and he used to curse like a trooper.

The May Fair used to block the road by the Bullring, but I remember it snowing once on the 17th May and they couldn't have the fair, nor could the customers get to the shop.

The farmers and people used to bring in their eggs for us to sell, and butter from the farms, which we would cut to the customer's requirements. The farmers used to buy 20lb bars of salt for when they were killing a pig so that they could make the bacon, and would give us the spare ribs, which were delicious. They used to bring ducks, pheasants, and salmon from Whitney Court – they used to supply the shop when they had plenty, and used to ring up and ask 'How many do you want?' The salmon would weigh between 10 and 20lbs, but I reckon the best size was about 14lb. They had to be spring fish, early *in the year was best, and we always had Wye salmon on Good Friday.*

The flour was milled locally from W. Harris at Clock Mill, and we used to pack it up ourselves, also rice, soda, currants, sultanas and demerera sugar. We had to measure out vinegar in pint pots and used to have to take the scales to the police station for them to be checked and stamped. Loaves used to be sold by weight – 1lb, 2lbs and 4lbs. There were two big ovens and we used to make up the fires overnight so the bread could be baked first thing in the morning. **Mac Maddy**

Mrs Maddy said that Mr Maddy never had a holiday. He had to work all the time, especially after his father and uncle retired, both of whom had served in the First World War, his father suffering from shellshock and carrying some shrapnel wounds.

In those days they used to buy direct from suppliers, buying 16lbs of tea at a time that they used to blend 'to suit the water of Hay' and they were packed and labelled 'Black and White' tea. Once companies started being taken over they wanted to reduce the number of lines and sell in bulk, which is what contributed to the end of the local grocer. **Mrs Maddy**

Maddys sold everything. My mother bought from there. Even David went up there with a note — well, there was no cars around, not during the war. When he was three he'd go up to Maddys, except he'd go up

there and get a pound of sausages and give them to the first dog he met. During the war you could go to one shop and buy your rations and we used to go to Maddys. **Emma Dunn**

KILVERT'S HOTEL

Dr Hugh Powell's surgery was in the Kilvert, remembers **Mac Maddy;** and he used to be driven around by a chauffeur in an Austin 12. **Mary Davies** remembers being taken to see Dr Powell at Kilvert's because she was bitten on the face by a dog, but the only treatment she remembers was being given some chocolate! She was only about three.

Kilvert's was a doctor's. That was Dr Powell's for as long as I could remember until Mr Morelli bought it, more or less. (Terry Salter converted the building to a hotel before selling it to Mr. Morelli.) That was his house and his surgery. The main part, that was the house and the side of it, that was the surgery. I always went to Dr Powell. I went there with a cyst on my eye and he just stood me in front of a mirror and cut it off. No anaesthetic. He asked me to hold the cotton wool and just slit it open, lanced it, and he said to my mother later, 'Where's that girl of yours?' Mother said 'Gone to the pictures'. I was thirteen. He said 'They do say "No sense, no feeling". She hasn't got any'. And mother said, 'I know'. I had a big bandage round it. Paid him half a crown.

I had to go twice. I went on the Monday and he had a look at it and he said 'If it doesn't burst come back'. So I went back on the Thursday with another half a crown. We couldn't afford it. If kids had pneumonia they'd send for my mother and my mother'd put steamed kettles going.

People have come to our door. 'Is your mum there?'. 'Yes'. 'Can I speak to her?'. They wouldn't tell me what it was, but it was to borrow clean sheets because they needed to call the doctor and they didn't have no clean sheets. She'd give them but she'd never have them back. No wonder she had 32 pair of sheets when she died – brand new, in cellophane, and towels and pillow slips. **Emma Dunn**

There was often a boxing booth outside Kilvert's [at the May Fair].... Where the antique shop is now at the bottom of the Bullring used to be Maddys the grocer's and Max Maddy lives in Cusop now. He was the son of one of the two brothers who were grocers there. **Rex Jones**

And of course there was another house which was used to cure skins, the other side of the Kilvert car park. Mr Price has renovated it and put a lot of it back, and that was an old warehouse and on the roof in those days instead of sort of windows there were sky-lights with wooden vents in to allow the air to dry the skins. I think that went on to Mr Greenway, who was in Hay. They used to cure skins and buy and sell and that there.

In my day as a youngster Hay was full of poachers. We had one who reckoned he was so good at the job he only had to walk in the field and shout

Castle Square 1930

loud enough and all the rabbits dropped dead! I wouldn't dare to do it because there were a dozen or more poachers who did nothing else really. They did have jobs, but they didn't work very often. They were more active at night. The rabbits were a nuisance, but it's amazing how some farmers didn't like poachers on their land. It was before myxamotosis and there were plenty of rabbits about. I remember going to a fire near Rhydspence, a house, at 5.00 in the morning. Having got to the fire, you looked up the bank and there wasn't a space more than a foot square where there wasn't rabbits sitting, they were all over the place, rabbit holes everywhere. **Reg Lewis**

The jazz festival at Kilvert's was good, but there were complaints about the noise. **Jennifer Lawrence**

THE BRITISH LEGION CLUB

…where the British Legion is now, at the back there was a bakery. Old man named Pitt did the baking. **Rex Jones**

The fire station was near the Castle Lane, just above the British Legion Club. **Reg Lewis**

The British Legion was the Conservative Club originally and a baker's above that. **Emma Dunn**

I've been on the British Legion committee for over 20 years and the oldest member, I think, is Reg Lewis. He was born and bred here. Grandpa was a master

The opening of Maddy's new bakery, Bell Bank, Hay c.1880. William Pitt snr. on left, unknown in middle, William Pitt jnr (Lily Pitt's father) on right

builder and a sanitary inspector on Builth Council for years. Dad had three sons. One went to Australia, one was a schoolteacher, he went to London. **Charlie Evans**

MARKET STREET

There was a chap called Mr Bondi who used to buy rabbits for 1d and dry the skins in a place behind the antique 'supermarket' – it smelt horrible. **Mac Maddy**

Mr and Mrs Elkington both remembered Donald Hume; his factory was called The Atom Factory because it caught fire so often.

Donald Hume used to come to Hay in a great big car that filled Castle Street. My brother worked for him for a time, I think it was an electrical shop, and he had two fires there. He married a girl from Kington, which is why he came to Hay, and wanted to be a pilot. **Lily Pitt**

Mona Morgan worked at the small factory owned by Donald Hume where they made coils and switches for electric fires.

This was some time in the latter part of the 1940s. Hume married Cynthia Wright of Kington and they had a daughter. He didn't live in Hay but used to stay at the Wye Hotel, which was a beautiful hotel. He was friendly with Alfie Gittins, who ran the hotel and used to stay in with the Gittins' children if they went out for an evening. He used to wear an Air Force uniform and had flashy cars, but he was a very nice man. I can't imagine him doing what he did later on. He had a little dog called Toby. He liked to give the impression he was a pilot, and presumably he did fly the plane that dropped Setty's body in the Marsh! **Mona Morgan**

Round by the castle wall, Donald Hume had a place. They reckon they used to have all sorts of vehicles coming in there and disappearing in a couple of days. Didn't he chop a body up and drop it somewhere? **Rex Jones**

We had a couple of fires in Market Street when Donald Hume had the factory there. If you remember, Donald Hume was the man accused of murder in the Setty case and served a life sentence in jail. When he came out he was in Hay again because I saw him for a short while. We had two fires in the time that he was in Market Street and of course a lot of the locals think that the fires were sort of lit by him because he was seen in the factory a few seconds before the fires started, and in minutes the fire was right out through the roof and everything was going like mad. The only mistake he made was that we were on duty at the fire station and we were there in about two minutes, much to everyone's surprise.

Well, Hume was a man who came to Hay, he claimed to be an ex-RAF pilot. He wore RAF clothing and had RAF wings. I got to know him quite well. He was staying in the Wye Hotel in Hay, which is the Penny Bun now, and I used to see him going in the Blue Boar because at that time I came home from the Air Force and I was living in, I don't know if it's the same, it was called Radnor House, next door to the Vicarage. I used to see him in there. Well, he had these fires, and he married a lady from Kington. This man said he was a car dealer and he used to deal in cars, Hume, and he was known in some parts of the world as Brown. Well, this happened and this body was pulled out of the Romney Marshes. Now, Hume said he had a pilot's license. He'd never been in the RAF and this is what the papers said, after. They dropped the body in the marshes and they'd got pulled out of the marshes. He was tried – he got away with it in the first case, and then he went abroad and he shot a bank teller in Holland. He was put in there for life and then he wrote a story in the Daily Mirror *in which he confessed that he had murdered Setty and he said why he had done it. He served his life sentence and then he came back and got involved in some trouble again and finished up in jail in Great Britain but he lived in Market Street for quite a long time, where the antique shop is, where there's more than one shop, you know.*

It was previously Mr Bondi, who used to buy and sell rabbit skins years ago and cured hides and things. That's going back to when I was a child. I remember him well and his daughter, Brenda. I think she went to Market Harborough. We weren't allowed in there. **Reg Lewis**

Where the antique market is was Mr Bondi's who was a furrier and he was Jewish and the most wonderful man you've ever met. He used to come up to the cinema on a Saturday. Didn't matter how many kids were there, he'd say to Mr Madigan, 'Count them in and I'll pay.' He had a brother in Belgium but he died in 1939 when the war started. Then his wife kept it on, but she wasn't like him. And he went right back to where Hebbards is. Where Hebbards is now back off the pavement used to be two shops with grass in front and railings round. They used to be a fish shop and a shoe repair shop. **Emma Dunn**

When you come along Market Street, there was a shop used to deal in things like animal fat and candle tallow and that sort of thing. **Rex Jones**

The timber-framed building [Carlisles] on the right is the most complete in Hay and dates from early in the 17th century. This shop was formerly the only pre-Booth second-hand bookshop in the town, dark, confusingly cluttered but often extremely rewarding to the persistent searcher. **Walking Round Hay**

[Richard Booth] used to buy books by the tea chest full but there was a bookseller called Michael White who lived in virtual poverty and he used to look through the ones Richard threw out and sell them, and he made a living like that. He lived in what is Carlisle's now, but I can't remember what was in Chattels.

Then there was a grocer's with a sign saying 'Open Tuesday's 9-11am'. The antique shop sold antiques even then, and was an upholsterer as well. Then there was a grocer's shop that used to supply other grocers, it could have been called Greens, I think. **Eleri Golesworthy**

At the very end where the car park is now there used to be a shop there that did teas and they used to do faggots and peas. That was Jones the Tavern which was at the end of Market Street. Loads of people did faggots and peas. Your mum would do the potatoes and that was a meal. You took a basin and sometimes you only had to pay sixpence for them or a shilling. They were out of this world, not like the faggots now. It was a real treat. Then they came round the corner to Market Street and then they had a little sweet shop. Next door to that was Frank Powells, who was another sweet shop with grocery and they sold, oh, all sorts of things. Then next to that somebody actually lived in there – Sheila Like's, and then next to Sheila Like's the Greenways lived and they used to buy anything like rabbit skins and all that sort of thing. **Emma Dunn**

HIGH TOWN

In 1835, *Pigot's Directory* shows this to be the centre of trade in Hay, with all sorts of shops around the brand new market hall, built by Mr Enoch in 1833. They were the following:

Walter Cornstable, baker, confectioner and grocer
James Davies, bookseller and library
*   (the first library in Hay)*
Samuel Morris, bookseller and stationer
Thomas Bevan Watkins, bookseller and stationer
James Davies, boot and shoe maker
David Pritchard, boot and shoe maker
Mary Jones, butcher
William Jones, butcher
Nathaniel Morgan, butcher
Luke Price, butcher
Joseph Lewis, chemist and druggist
Henry Biddle, grocer and linen and woollen draper
William Enoch, grocer and dealer in sundries,
*   linen and woollen draper*
Sampson Higgins, grocer, ironmonger and tallow
*   chandler*
William Lloyd, grocer and dealer in sundries
John Games, hairdresser, and longest serving town
*   crier (or Sergeant-at-Mace) at a total of 43 years*
Eleanor Games, straw hat maker, his sister or wife
Ann Forster, milliner, straw hat maker and dressmaker
Ann Lloyd, milliner and dressmaker
Richard Bromage, glazier
Henry Biddle, saddler
William Lloyd, saddler
James Farr Higgins, skinner
Samuel Morris, stone mason
Margaret Vincett, straw hat maker
Richard Jones, vet
William Masters, basket maker

The number of straw hat makers shows that Hay was somewhat behind the times. William Cobbett, in his *Cottage Economy*, had lamented the decline of the English straw hat making industry several years earlier, when higher quality straw hats (known as Leghorn's) were being imported from Italy. Cobbett suggested methods of improving quality, but the English industry gradually declined. In the early 19th century nearly everyone, male and female, wore straw hats.

THE BUTTERMARKET

Of course there was nothing in the Buttermarket then because it was all closed up.
Eleri Golesworthy

This was built originally by W. Enoch, the grocer, in 1833, and this probably encouraged the building of the Old Town Hall in 1835, by Sir Joseph Bailey.

The Warren Club restored the Butter Market in the middle of the town. Years ago it was taken over by Mr George Keylock, who had a sort of Army and Navy type shop in Hay. It was eventually taken over by Jones the chemist as a stores for his shop. The space between all the pillars was bricked up and it was sealed up so one of our first projects was to restore the Butter Market and we spent quite a lot of money and did it all up. It was a good many years ago. **Rex Jones**

Bon Marche

The Buttermarket during the war was all blocked in because the railings were taken away. It was an egg station, where they brought all the eggs in the war because, remember, eggs were rationed. The farmers brought them in and they'd be sold wherever they had to go because in Hay there was no problem getting eggs. My mother kept her own chickens. But that was the egg station where they were graded and all that sort of thing. **Emma Dunn**

…just past the Buttermarket, on the left is a small area of pavement four or five feet wide and twenty long. In the last century this tiny site was the location of a house in which lived a shoemaker with his family of four children! **Walking Round Hay**

THE OLD TOWN HALL

The original Town Hall had five rooms, for various commodities, and was set up by the inhabitants of Hay before the reign of James I. There was an early 17th-century court case involving the bailiff of the castle, Thomas Gwatkin, who was illegally renting out the rooms to David Morris for £5.15s.0d a year. The court leet met here.

The present hall was built on the site of the medieval building two years after William Enoch had built a new Butter Market building at his own expense in 1833, Enoch was the premier grocer in Hay. The Town Hall was the responsibility of Sir Joseph Bailey, lord of the manor. He collected the market tolls, as did his son until 1893, when the tolls were bought by the Urban District Council for £100.

Roman Catholic services were held in the upper room from the late 1920s until 1968, when they were moved to the old Presbyterian church in Belmont Road, which is still the Roman Catholic church. Earlier, the Independants and the Wesleyans had held services here. In 1842 Mr D. Griffiths, who had been a missionary in Madagascar, came to live in Hay and began to preach in the Town Hall, where he gathered a large congregation despite opposition from local rowdies. In 1845 the Ebenezer Chapel, now the Globe Gallery, was built for him, but he left the area several years later to concentrate on translating the Bible.

In 1891 the Masonic Lodge met in the upper room – they later moved into the school buildings in Brecon Road, which they still use. The basement was a corn market. The keeper of the Town Hall was James Evans. The Hon. Sec. of the Loyal Hay Lodge of Freemasons No 2,382 was James Henry Tutton *(Kelly's Directory).*

In the 1990s Edward Folkard, sculptor, made a statue of Henry VII, which is now in place on one wall of the Old Town Hall. It was paid for by business consultant Steve Felgate, when he moved his business to Edinburgh and Windsor. The statue was unveiled by George Melly the jazz star.

I can remember when we had the VE party in the Market Hall. My mother did all the garlands and that. We had visitors up there and we hadn't got a cup in the house to give them a cup of tea – they had to come over to the Market Hall for a cup of tea. Everything was down the Market Hall. **Emma Dunn**

I saw the Cheese Market [the other name for the Old Town Hall] being used to sell cheese once but it was for a programme. There's a wonderful room upstairs there that used to be the Council Chamber. **Eleri Golesworthy**

The present Market Place below the castle wall is not the original location of Hay's markets; this lay to the east of this site for until late last century much of the square was covered with buildings, Castle Lane and Market Street meeting at a point opposite the War Memorial. **Walking Round Hay**

The War Memorial used to be in the middle of the square, and there was a big building there that has since been demolished, the Market Tavern. **Lily Pitt**

There used to be a brilliant procession through the town on 11th November and there was a growing section of cadets and they had a wonderful brass band. **Charlie Evans**

My mother was the luckiest woman – to have four boys in the army and they all came back. My mother didn't go to bed for three months because my one brother, they said he was missing, we had a telegram to say he was missing in Italy. What had happened, the Americans had picked him up and not reported it. My father used to tell the Yanks in the pubs they're like Fred Carno's army and what was Fred Carno's army? A bloody circus! My mother sat in the window for three months during the night and slept during the day in case he came home. Then they found out he'd been injured in both legs but he was all right. The other one, he came back from Dunkirk. He was only in this country three months and they sent him to the Far East. David [my son] was three months old I think when he went. I had Susan when he got back. He didn't get back until the end of '46. He got made an officer in Burma because they'd lost so many. He was only a sergeant but they made him up. He was a regular soldier. He did his seven years in the army. My other brother did fifteen years in the army and then he got killed on a motorbike. **Emma Dunn**

The Market Tavern [A. Williams]. Mrs Bidmead made faggots with peas for 2d here. The town's elite left it late and by the back way. **Wisps of Hay**

The Monument was put up in 1921 and moved to its present position sometime in the 1950s. The Market Square was the bus terminal where the Western Welsh buses started every morning, taking people to Brecon. Originally Fred Crooks drove the bus to Llandrindod Wells twice a day as that was the place to go then, and only later did it go to Brecon. A different bus went to Hereford – the Hereford Red and White and the Midland Red. **Dick Elkington**

There were more buses in those days, including one from Cheltenham, going on to Tenby.
Eleri Golesworthy

1 HIGH TOWN

This is a listed building known as Compton House. It houses Oxfam and Hay Fever antique shop. It is late Georgian in date with probable 17th-century origins. In 1891 Henry John Stephens had his draper's and outfitter's here, and he also had a boot and shoe warehouse at 20 High Town, a building that seems to have disappeared.

Oxfam was the doctor's surgery, with a Dr Trumper when my husband was a boy. **Eleri Golesworthy**

I left school at 14 or 15 and was apprenticed to Pugh the draper's where they sold materials by the yard, and clothes and shoes. **Mona Morgan**

The small shop next to Oxfam, Pughs had that as well. They were bigger than Golesworthys. Pughs prices were reasonable. I can remember buying a suit from Pughs. My brother sent me £5 from Palestine in 1934. He was in the army. They were out there when the Jews and Arabs were rioting and they're still rioting! He went out there in 1933. He sent me £5 and I was most upset – the bank charged me a shilling for changing it. I bought a suit with that money from Pughs and it was London tan. That's what they called the colour, and I got it for £5, shoes and all. **Emma Dunn**

2 HIGH TOWN

A listed building, now occupied by Havard's grocer's shop (Londis). It is early 19th century. In 1891 Edwin Browning, grocer and provision dealer, had his shop here, *(Kelly's Directory)*, and this may be the site of Mr Enoch's grocer's shop in the early 19th century, though it's impossible to be certain.

Mrs Elkington came to Hay when she was 11, moving from Essex because of the war, as her mother had originally come from Hay. They moved into what is now Havard's grocers and her mother ran a laundry and dry cleaning business from there. The house was in a terrible state, with an outside toilet.

That was Mills, the grocer's shop, where Mark Havard is now and then during the war, in Mills's day it was a collecting depot for a laundry. It went back to being a grocer's after they gave up the laundry. **Emma Dunn**

3 High Town

This is also listed, as part of the row, and is early 19th century, refronted in the late 19th century. It is now the post office, and in 1891 it was a draper's shop belonging to James Morris, who also had a draper's shop in Lion Street, as well as being a grocer and corn merchant at 18 High Town *(Kelly's Directory)*.

The Post Office was Lloyds Bank but they did a deal with the National Westminster, who took over all their customers in Hay, whilst the Lloyds Bank took over the Nat West customers in Llandrindod Wells.
Dick Elkington

During the War, G.I.s were billeted here. The building was owned by the War Office until 1942. I was a postwoman for 34 years, with 2 deliveries a day in those days. **Lily Pitt**

4 High Town

It, together with 'adjoining premises', were used as a dissenters' meeting house. Mrs Susannah Swetman, widow of John Swetman, mercer, and her father Thomas Howells, flannel manufacturer, with Nathaniel Morgan of Ross-on-Wye, draper, were all mentioned in a mortgage of No. 4 in 1815. Thomas and Susannah were known to be Quakers. Thomas Howells owned the spinning and weaving factory attached to Grants in Castle Street. Susannah was a trustee of Goff's School from 1813.

The licence for the meeting house was granted in 1813. The preacher was David Davies, who also headed the charity school which started at the same time, and who may have been associated with Lady Huntingdon's College at Trevecca. He was listed in the churchwardens' rate assessment book of 1825 as a preacher, and died in 1848 and is buried in Hay churchyard. The congregation later split up and joined other chapels.

There is an entrance to the back of the building via a courtyard, and this area was occupied by Hay Makers before they moved to Arvona Gallery in St John's Place. It is now partially occupied by Brian Wiggington, antique restorer and dealer. Pembertons New Bookshop is the present occupier of this building, which is listed, and has an early 19th-century frontage (although the origins of the building are said to go back to 1690).

…and the bookshop next door, that was all troops. I can remember that being a hardware shop.
Emma Dunn

5 High Town

Now the Hayloft Gallery.

6 High Town

This is now Monica's clothes shop, and is another listed building. When the listing was taking place, in 1987, the shop was occupied by Quinto of Hay. It is early 19th century, and was shown on the 1847 tithe map.

There used to be a billiard hall up above, but during the war it got taken over for troops – they lived in there. Briggs was the cheapest outfitters, where Monicas is now. **Emma Dunn**

7 HIGH TOWN

This building dates from the early 19th century and is also listed. It was formerly the Three Horseshoes Inn. By 1891 it had become a chemist run by John Lutwyche Davies and it was the chemist's shop involved in the Armstrong murder case. It currently trades under the name of R.M. Jones Chemist.

There was also a grocer's shop called Burtons which was half of the current chemist's shop and used to be the Indian-China shop. **Mac Maddy**

I can remember when they called Burtons 'India and China' because of the teas they used to sell. Loose teas and the sugar was loose then. They used to weigh the sugar in a bag. Nothing was prepacked then. They used to slice all bacon and corned beef. They used to have corned beef in big tins and then slice it. You'd buy for that day but later on when money got better my mother always had a stock of everything. She used to make all her own jam and she used to pickle everything, I think. **Emma Dunn**

A lot of people used to go to the chemist for advice about different things. Doctors in those days had to be paid. The chemist was where it is now – a man who was there for many years was Mr Jack Heard who was what you call the pharmacist today and Mr Heard went back to the days when Davies was the chemist there and the well-known Armstrong case. He stayed there until he was a very old man. Many people went to him for advice because it was cheaper than going to the doctor. The nurses mainly saw to births and things like that and they used to get called in if somebody had died to lay them out. My grandfather was the undertaker in the town. **Reg Lewis**

The chemist used to have a side door with a step that always used to open at quarter to nine at night – because the doctors didn't close at six o'clock like they do now – for anybody that had a prescription, for about an hour. It was Davies before then because when David was born we had difficulty feeding him and they used to sell baby food called Davies's which they made themselves. It was a sort of paste but David liked it.

Mr Nutt that used to be at the chemist was equally as good as any doctor because when I was having Susan I went to him. I hated the doctors. Rather than go to the doctor I'd rather go to Mr Nutt and he had a look at only my eyes and that and he thought I was going to have Brights disease, kidney, but it wasn't that. I had to go in hospital and have an operation and he knew something was wrong. My mother in the end got Dr Malkinson and they lived in Staunton. She sent me in hospital.

Mr Nutt had a man there; he was very old. He used to be with Davies the chemist. You could go there and ask him for something, show him what was wrong. He'd give you something and it was gone. They were wonderful. **Emma Dunn**

Of those 32 licensed houses, only 9 survive – and in June 1962, the landlords of each turned up to oppose an application to the Licensing Bench by the town's only chemist for permission to sell alcohol. The landlords of Hay protested, pointing out that they all had to take second jobs to make ends meet. One worked in the Signal-box at the Railway Station; another had just relinquished the job (which his predecessor had also held) of driving a Western Welsh bus 'twixt Hay and Brecon; yet another formerly holding a license had also been a lawyer's clerk, whilst his wife – an Aberystwyth Primitive Methodist at that, held the fort at opening time; the former owner of the second largest hotel was in an almshouse and even the Court Reporter had failed to make a 'go of it' at what must be regarded as the premier hostelry, at a time when his family owned it. The chemist lost his application. **Wisps of Hay**

8 HIGH TOWN

This is a listed building, known as Crown House, and is early 19th century in origin. It is now the upper half of the chemist's shop. In 1891 the Misses Elizabeth Ann and Emma Garrett were milliners and drapers here *(Kelly's Directory)*.

9 HIGH TOWN

This is now Shepherd's ice cream parlour, and was previously Hay Prints. It is a listed building, late Georgian in origin, and is shown on the 1847 tithe map. It has been a fishmonger's or butcher's at some time, as the marble slabs are still in place in the window.

…then where Chris Powell was, another grocer's shop. Nobody went to supermarkets then – they didn't have cars – they didn't have supermarkets! And they used to weigh the butter and cut off big pieces of butter. I mean, you could go in the store and ask for two ounces of butter, and during the war you only got an ounce of butter and four ounces of margarine or something. The biggest grocer's was Stars.
Emma Dunn

This was Star Supply Stores – a general grocer's.
Dick Elkington

10 HIGH TOWN

This is now Mayall's the watchmaker and jeweller's shop. In 1891 Alfred Henry Mayall, watchmaker, had his shop here, and his son Billy kept the shop until his death in the late 1990s, an astonishing two generations spanning almost 100 years of the shop's existance. The shop is still owned by the Mayall family.

Mayall's have been there since year dot. I remember his father and mother living there and he had a sister Joyce and another brother who died when he was 50. Mrs Mayall his wife lives in Bear Street now. It's been nothing but a jeweller's shop and there were only two jeweller's shops in Hay. One Mayall girl got married to a boy from Llowes Court. He got killed in the war. For a small place, we lost a lot of boys.
Emma Dunn

Mr Mayall's was still there, and I took my watch to him once but my husband told me to take it away again and I had to identify which one was mine, they were in such a muddle. **Eleri Golesworthy**

The grandfather was the Parade Marshall on Civic Sunday and Armistice Day and used to wear a bowler hat and carry a walking stick. **Dick Elkington**

11 HIGH TOWN

This is now the estate agent McCartneys. It is listed, along with Mayall's, above. The buildings are late Georgian, and shown on the 1847 tithe map.

There was a shop where they sit now for the Ice Cream shop, run by a man called Nobby, which sold all sorts of plastic stuff. **Eleri Golesworthy**

Nobby Wilkins had a shop called the Bon Marche by the end of the Cheese Market (since demolished). The Bon Marche sold pots and pans, brooms, paraffin, etc and he later moved into McCartney's estate agents as it is now, and opened the shop there after having lived in it as a house, and he then lived in the cottage at the back. Before that it was an ice cream shop called Cockshaws. He used to go round on his bike selling ice cream. **Dick Elkington**

I can remember it being a barber's and a sweet shop and an ice cream shop. On the corner where they've got that statue used to be a hardware shop, used to be Nobby Williams', Bon Marche. He moved behind Sunderlands. He had that all fitted out. You could go there for a pint of paraffin in a pop bottle which you can't do now. **Emma Dunn**

12 HIGH TOWN

This is now the HSBC Bank, formerly the Midland, which opened in 1921. In 1926 the manager was John Edward Reese (*Kelly's Directory*). It stands on the site of the Fountain Inn, which was licensed from 1830-40, and was demolished around 1870. After it closed as a pub, it was used as a bottling plant for soft drinks, run by Thomas Stokoe, the local chemist and vet. He was also a grocer, and agent for W. & A. Gilbey, wine and spirit merchants. He also ran the Crown in Broad Street. In 1864 Thomas Stokoe was noted in the *Hereford Times* as having won the anatomy medal in examinations at the Veterinary College in Edinburgh, and he was classed first, with medal, in the general exam. He had been assistant to the druggist Mr B. Hadley.

There was Stokoe's Bottling Plant at the back of the HSBC Bank. A Mrs Morgan lived in a cottage there opposite the yard, and the British Legion bought the yard but never built on it and later sold it to Nobby Wilkins [since demolished]. **Dick Elkington**

Eric Pugh's [the electrical shop on the Pavement] used to be the dole office. I can remember a queue from there right up to the Midland Bank, only the Midland bank was Stokoes, a wholesale wine store. That was during the 30s. Everyone was out of work. Jean Prendergast's auntie worked there. **Emma Dunn**

13 High Town

This is now the lower part of Mike Bullock's bookshop, but was recently a separate property, housing the Meridian Gallery for a time. In 1891 John Lewis Pugh, bootmaker, lived here *(Kelly's Directory)*. In 1987 it was known as Ye Olde Curiosity Shop, and had previously been a bakery.

This was Herbert Stephens' bakery and tea shop. **Dick Elkington**

Where Mike Bullock's got his two shops now, well the first shop was a little tea shop. They used to serve teas and bread and cakes which they made themselves. **Emma Dunn**

14 High Town

This is now the main part of Mike Bullock's bookshop, Hay-on-Wye Booksellers, formerly called River Wye Booksellers. This is a listed timber-framed building dating from the 17th century.

In 1891 Septimus Williams was a tailor here *(Kelly's Directory)*, assisted by William James McCarthy, who was also involved in the running of the Ebenezer Chapel at the top of Newport Street *(Wisps of Hay)*.

This was a barber's. **Dick Elkington**

That shop I can remember being a chemist and they lived there as well. **Emma Dunn**

15 High Town, Paris House

This is now the Red Cross Shop. It is a listed building with early 19th-century origins. It is said to have some timber framing on the upper floor. In 1891 Thomas William Evans, saddler and harness maker, had his shop here *(Kelly's Directory)*. Up to the 1990s the shop was an old-fashioned haberdasher's. When the owners retired, in 1993 or 94, it was taken over by an antiques shop, but this proved to be the front for a counterfeiting operation. Desmond Boys, an unemployed master printer, made the false bank notes; police eventually seized notes with a face value of £324,000. His son, David Boys, was the antiques dealer, and had photographed the £20 notes for printing; notes with a face value of £39,820 were found in the boot of his car. David Boys was also found to be making pornographic films.

The Red Cross shop was Jessica's haberdashery – incredible corsets, and then it was an antique shop – the owner was a lovely girl – I'm sure she didn't know what was going on. **Jennifer Lawrence**

The Red Cross was Gwilliams. I can remember I used to buy David little suits from there, 3/11. **Emma Dunn**

16 High Town, Grove House

This is now Mark Westwood's bookshop, and is a listed building dating back to the late 17th century, with late Georgian alterations. Before Mark Westwood moved here, in the early 1990s, it was a hardware shop. In 1891 it was home to Tom Parry a butcher's *(Kelly's Directory)*.

17 HIGH TOWN

This is known as Scotland House, and is also a listed building. Like No. 16, it is late 17th century in origin, altered in the early 19th century. In 1987 it was The Tea Shop and Just Hair.

That used to be a paper shop. Ferris's had that. They were called Ferris's first but then Mrs Watkins had it who was a daughter of Ferris's. **Emma Dunn**

18 HIGH TOWN, OSCAR'S

This restaurant has retained the name Oscar's, though it has changed hands more than once since it started. Back in 1987, though, it was called the Haywain. It is a listed building, late Georgian in origin, and shown on the 1847 tithe map. In 1891 James Morris, grocer and corn merchant, owned this property and also the draper's at 3 High Town and another in Lion Street *(Kelly's Directory)*.

19 HIGH TOWN

This is now Caer Gwydion, which sells Celtic style fancy goods. Before that, it was Mark Westwood's shop, and before that, according to the assistant, it was a fancy goods shop again.

Deesons used to be on the corner where that jewellery shop is now. Deesons was another dress shop and then Pughs was next door where Oscar's is and then when Pughs gave up Miss Deason moved next door as well. **Emma Dunn**

There was a hat shop opposite where Oxfam is run by a Mrs Deason. **Eleri Golesworthy**

20 HIGH TOWN

In 1891 Henry John Stephens had his boot and shoe warehouse here and he also had a draper's and outfitters at 1 High Town *(Kelly's Directory)*. By the numbering this should make the two buildings very close together, but there is no trace of 20 High Town on the ground. Enquiries at Clee, Tomkinson and Francis drew a blank, as their address is 5/6 St John's Place.

APPENDIX
THE ANCIENT ORDER OF FORESTERS IN HAY

The Foresters in Hay are mentioned three times in William Plomer's abridgement of the *Diary of Francis Kilvert* and once in Dafydd Ifan's transcription of the complete diary entries for June-July 1870. In the latter there is a very detailed description of the Foresters' Fete at Hay, to which Kilvert was invited by Mr Allen. This and the entries in the *Hay Parish Magazine* and the *Hereford Times* throws light on a now forgotten aspect of life in The Hay.

THE FRIENDLY SOCIETY MOVEMENT
IN THE 19TH CENTURY

For small businessmen, junior managers, office workers and artizans, even short term illness threatened destitution, for without good health it was difficult to reverse the downward spiral of impoverishment that led in the first case to the Work or Poor House. The final ignominy came with burial in an unmarked pauper's grave, or worse still in a communal burial pit. Fear of parish relief induced a preoccupation with respectable independence, with its associated self-esteem and standing in the surrounding community.

As industrialisation developed in the 18th century men grouped together to form Friendly Societies, each member contributing a weekly sum to a common fund. From this fund contributors could draw support in times of need; the better organised societies often would meet the cost of medical attention and ultimately the cost of a 'respectable' if humble burial.

Another aspect of the Friendly Societies was the use of oaths and the special clothing termed 'Regalia'. This was not out of line with then current behaviour, for the legal system depended on much oath taking and people regularly wore uniforms particular to the function being performed.

There were several national orders of Friendly Societies including the Manchester Unity of Oddfellows, the Templars and the Rechabites, amongst which there was a considerable rivalry.

As a regular contributor of verse to the *Hereford Times* Francis Kilvert may well have read the issue for Saturday 30 January 1869 that allows us to see Victorian Forestry in its heyday. The paper devoted two columns running to over 2,000 words to the 12th Anniversary Dinner of Hereford's oldest Court Maiden at the Foresters' Hall, The Old Harp, 126 Widemarsh Street Hereford, where 160 members and their friends sat down to dinner. At this event various speakers proposed and responded to 15 toasts that included the Bishop and Clergy of the diocese.

FORESTERS IN HAY-ON-WYE:
THE HEREFORDSHIRE DISTRICT CONNECTION

The opening of the railway between Brecon and Hereford in 1864 provided regular transport between Hay and the middle Wye villages. At that time Hay was a trading centre in an extensive agricultural area.

Hereford City was, by the standards of the day, large and self important, with a great cathedral and many regional connections. For example the weekly *Hereford Times*, with an advertised circulation of 12,000 per week in 1876, served a vast area in the Marches, South and Mid Wales, carrying international, national and local news of regional interest.

At the time the Order of Foresters was expanding rapidly. By 1869 there were 17 courts or formal gatherings in the Herefordshire District, with a total membership of 1,345.

In 1866 the Herefordshire District Officers came to Hay to open Court Perseverance number 4906 – for each local unit, court, lodge or tent of a national order was numbered. Three years later, with 65 members, Perseverance was one of the larger courts in the district, with sufficient business to meet on alternate Mondays.

According to the Ancient Order of Foresters (AOF) Directory 1869/70, Perseverance met at the Wheatsheaf Lion Inn with J. Wall of Gravel Street as Secretary. This should read Wheat Sheaf Inn, Lion Street, and Gravel Street is now Chancery Lane.

THE HAY AND WYE SIDE DISTRICT

In 1869 another court was opened at Eardisley, number 5381 Integrity at the Tram Inn, with 26 members and J. Jay, an Eardisley tailor, as secretary. It met every four weeks. Eardisley was a rapidly developing hamlet that served a large rural area, whilst a new community was being created at the wagon works of the Brecon and Merthyr Railway which was then running the Hereford, Hay and Brecon Railway.

It was natural for the two courts (total funds £150) to found, on 24 November 1869, the Hay and Wye Side District.

In 1872 Perseverance had a change of secretary. Henry John Moro, of 40 Lion Street, took over, and for the time being the court continued to meet at the Wheatsheaf. However, in the following year Perseverance moved its meeting place down Lion Street to the room over the Red Lion at number 41. This room seems to have been a public room for very many years; in 1765 it had been licenced for the Quakers to hold religious meetings when they held their Welsh national gathering in Hay.

Henry Moro was clearly a key figure in Hay 'Forestry'. By 1875 he was the District Secretary and Relieving Officer working with J. Jones, shoemaker of Castle Street who was District Chief Ranger, with G. Tilley as District Treasurer. The function of the Foresters' Relieving Officer was to provide cash to 'Brothers' – members – travelling in search of work. The traveller carried a 'travelling licence' which gave entry to courts *en route* and enabled the traveller to cash cheques issued by his own court to the value of either one shilling and sixpence or two shillings per day. Only one cheque could be cashed at a time. Clearly the Relieving Officer had a very responsible office for he had to be certain of the *bona fides* of the traveller as well as having access to cash from which to meet the cheques.

A 'clearance' or certificate of good standing enabled the traveller, once settled, to transfer to a local court without loss of benefit.

From his diary, it is known that Francis Kilvert was sympathetic to the travelling workman and that he assisted the Rector of Hay, W.L. Bevan, with the town branch of the Brecon Savings Bank. In a small community it seems safe to assume he would have known Brother Henry Moro and the other District Officers.

KILVERT AND THE FORESTERS' FETES

Francis Kilvert's published diary commences in 1870, five years after he had become curate in Clyro. It is clear from the diaries that Kilvert was familiar with the Foresters who, although meeting behind closed doors, were very self evident. He could not have avoided the Foresters' publicity typified by what I have called the 'Horden' poster of 1869.

This advertises the Foresters' Fete of 1869, the year before the Hay and Wyeside District as founded.

When the old print room of George Horden, Castle Street was converted into flats in 1996 various posters were found stuck to the walls advertising events in the town, including the Hay

Foresters' Anniversary. A photograph taken of the partially preserved poster before it was destroyed shows that it read, in a rich diversity of types:

(A)ncient Order of
(FO)RESTERS.
(Court? Pe)rseverance no.4906
(?) Members of the above Court intend holding their
(a)nnual
(AN)NIVERSARY,
(M)onday, July 12th, 1869,
at the
(?) Hall, Wheat Sheaf Inn, Hay
(?) will meet for business at half-past nine and at half-past Ten the
(GRA)ND PROCESSION
(?Fores)ters in full dress mounted on horseback,
Banners, Streamers and Regalia.
(??Br)ass Band is engaged for the whole of the day.
(M)embers will return to Forester's Hall to Dinner, when the attendance of visiting
(?) and Friends will be esteemed a favour.
(Din)ner 2s. 6d. EACH
(F)ORESTERS' BALL
will take ple(asure) (?)ing

KILVERT AT THE HAY FORESTERS' FETE: MONDAY 11 JULY 1870

On 7 July 1870, when visiting Mr and Mrs Haigh Allen at Clifford Priory Francis Kilvert was invited by Mr Henry Allen, aged 78, to luncheon at Oakfield, a large redbrick house to the west of The Hay, for the Foresters were coming to his house. This was held eight months after the new District came into being and seems to have been a grand event. Kilvert's *Diary* records the event:

A small school (at Clyro) this morning because of the Foresters' Fete in The Hay…. at 1.15 Mr Venables drove me to Oakfield to luncheon and to see the gathering and parade of the Foresters. We stopped a few minutes in the town at the corner near the Bank, and Father Ignatius's brother [Clavering Lynn] trotted by on a strawberry roan pony round the back street under the castle wall with a white and black spaniel at his heels.

The road was lively with people going to Oakfield to see the display.

As we got to the top of the long winding steep drive we heard a sudden burst of cheering, green flags waved and two policemen, who kept the iron gates, saluted as we drove through.

'You are too late for my eloquence' said Mr Allen as he greeted us. He had been making the Foresters a speech of which the burst of cheering we heard was the result and conclusion.

The front lawn of the house was lined and filled with the Foresters in green scarves, holding large green and white banners representing relief being brought to a distressed family. Two men on horseback dressed to represent Robin Hood and Little John in green tunics, white capes, white breeches and large red boots, with flat black caps and bugles slung over the shoulder, rode and rolled about on their carty bay horses looking very foolish and uncomfortable in fine borrowed feathers and false beards. They ordered the march round the grass plat before the front door.

First went Robin Hood and Little John rolling in their saddles like sacks, next straddled the Rifle Corps band blasting with their trumpets, and blowing out their cheeks till their eyes started, and the rear was brought up by the lurching banners and the men in green scarves marching to all sorts of time, and taking off their hats at the saluting point where Mr Allen stood, the corner of the house.

Then they took themselves off, the National Anthem having been played previously.

After 'lounging about' Kilvert with the gentry crowded into the house, 32 sitting down to a cold meal of salmon, chicken, salad, etc., 'and everything was very nice'. 'Mr Allen', Kilvert thought, 'was aged 80 and gets about and lives like other people and enjoys life'.

It is clear from Kilvert's description that there were several large coloured picture banners in the field, which each needed six Brothers to hold them still, two at the upright poles and one each on the four guy ropes. All the officers and initiated members would have worn the decorated sashes of their rank or green neck collars.

The Foresters' activity during Kilvert's time in Clyro and subsequently will be found in those *Hay Parish Magazines* that have survived at the St John's Rooms in Hay. The years available for review are 1879, 80, 82, 85, 86, 88, and 89.

The magazine commenced publication in 1875 being composed of a national illustrated religious journal of Bible stories and moral tales published by J. Erskine Clarke, London. To this 'core' was added a parish magazine by the Rector, Canon W.L. Bevan which was printed by George Horden, Castle Street. The whole cost 2d. Each monthly issue contained church news plus matters of topical interest in Hay parish – including train times. In the first surviving volume, that of 1879, it is clear that the Foresters' Fete was a well established event with a regular pattern.

The *Hereford Times* noted the Brothers assembled on 2 June outside the Foresters' Hall in Lion Street with the large banner of the Order and a band. There was a decorated triumphal arch over the street and oak branches framed the entrance to the Lodge above the Red Lion.

Like the Foresters' Fete in Hereford the event was washed out by rain although the morning had been beautifully fine. The parish magazine noted that Charlotte Mawn of Bridge Street was pushed or fell from some boarding and broke her arm, 'however she has since progressed favourably'.

The procession marched to the parish church for Divine Service, returned to their Lion Street Hall for a formal dinner and speeches before marching to a field for sports. (Even today the annual Remembrance Parade assembles in Lion Street with all the associated uniformed and other organisations. It marches east up Lion Street, makes a U-turn through St John's Place to march westwards down Market Street, High Town and Castle Street and on to St Mary's Church. The parade returns to town after the service).

In 1880 the fete was held on 24 May instead of the usual Whit Monday, when Mr G. Games took the chair at the dinner and Mr Lilwall lent his field at Nantyglaster. The 1882 event was held on 18 July. The Procession marched to the parish church for a sermon by Reverend Bevan's Curate, J.E. Lloyd, MA, who took as his text 1 Corinthians xvi, verse 13: 'Watch ye, stand fast in the faith, quit you like men, be strong'. They marched back to Lion Street, sitting down to an excellent dinner provided by the Secretary's wife, Mrs Moro of the Red Lion. Mr Crichton presided and after the usual toasts the Foresters went to Mr Maskell's field for athletic sports.

Three years later, 20 July 1885, Bevan himself preached and Lt Colonel W. Jones Thomas of Llanthomas presided. The day was deemed most successful although the attendance was small due to hay harvesting. Col. Thomas said that Foresters could not be congratulated on their punctuality, as he was forced to join toasts together. Mr R.T. Griffiths, Dr Applebee and Mr Lawdon organised and subscribed to the sports.

Bevan preached again in 1886, the service commencing at 11 o'clock. The dinner was held at the Drill Hall in Lion Street, and the athletics on the Sports Field on the Brecon Road.

Mr Lawdon took the chair in 1888 but this year the date was 3 September and the sports were held at 'The Cricket Field'. The Brecon Volunteer Company provided their brass band, the procession starting at 9 o'clock.

The order of Rechabites was a teetotal Friendly Society that drew inspiration from the 35th chapter of the book of Jeremiah where the sons of Rehab, although tempted by pots of wine, refused it, maintaining an oath of abstinence. The Biblical Rechabites also refused to be urbanised but lived in tents.

On 20 February 1889 the Parish magazine reported an 'Adult Tent' of the Order of Rechabites had held a public meeting at the Drill Hall. The Tent had thirty adult members with a junior Tent of forty-seven children. No doubt this teetotal friendly society had the special support of W.L. Bevan and would have been in conflict with the more liberal minded Foresters' group, although the latter did not welcome excess and were willing to turn out members who were not respectable.

Francis Kilvert, when he became Vicar of Bredwardine, became an honorary member of the local court Unity as reported in the *Hereford Times* on 9th November, who also reported the court's annual fete in May 1879 – covering the march from Moccas Court, the accompanying church service, the hymns sung and Kilvert's fitting sermon, and the sports where the reporter deprecated a certain amount of clownish behaviour by the local youths.

Apart from his wedding this was Francis Kilvert's last public event for he died suddenly on 23 September.

BIBLIOGRAPHY

Archaeologia Cambrensis, fourth series Vol XIV no LV, reissued by Richard Booth (Hay) as a pamphlet, 1980s

Banks, R.W. *The Early History of Hay and its Lordship*, July 1883

Brycheniog, various articles, especially Vol 28 1995-96

Clarke, Kate *The Book of Hay*, Logaston Press, 2000

Dictionary of National Biography

Fairs, Geoffrey L. *A History of Hay – The Story of Hay-on-Wye*, Phillimore, 1972

                Annals of a Parish: A short History of Hay-on-Wye, 1984

Jones, Theophilus *History of the County of Brecknock*, 1805-9

Morgan, Richard *An extent of the Lordship of Hay*

Morgan, W.E.T. *Hay and Neighbourhood*, 1932

Rees, William *The Medieval Lordship of Brecon*: a reprint from the Honourable society of Cymmrodorian in an address presented to William Rees by the Brecknock Society Brecon, 1968

Remfry, Paul Martin *Hay-on-Wye Castle*, 1995

                Castles of Breconshire, Logaston Press, 1999

Rose, Ronald *Walking Round Hay*, 1991

Salter, Mike *The Castles of Mid Wales*, Folly Publications, 1991

                The Old Parish Churches of Mid Wales, Folly Publications, 1991

Kelly's Directory for the years 1891 and 1926

Pigot's Directory for the year 1835

Wisps of Hay

Government rolls and charters etc

Powys County Council, Information about the listed buildings

Woolhope Society: various articles

Numerous more generalised histories

Also from Logaston Press

The Pubs of Leominster, Kington & North-West Herefordshire

by Ron Shoesmith and Roger Barrett
Price £9.95

This is a book about the social history of pubs in the north-west of Herefordshire. It includes—we hope—all the pubs that have existed over the past three hundred or so years, not just those that are still in existence. The area covered runs from the northern borders of Hereford with the Wye as the western boundary and an ill-defined eastern boundary amongst the villages to the east of the A49, reaching to the northern boundary of the county.

The book is structured around the roads that spread out from Hereford, as many of the inns and pubs once served travellers traversing the countryside. But first some details are given of the differences between pubs, inns and taverns, of local breweries and cider makers, and of changes over the years in licensing laws.

Then the story of the local pubs is given. Find out which one is renowned for fox and squirrel pie, of a man with a penchant for ashtrays in Leominster, appreciate why a Temperance Hotel may have been established just round the corner from the west end of Duke Street in Kington, of explosions in Kimbolton, of locals out-embarrassing punks, of landlords having to canoe packets of cigarettes to regulars, of pubs which have changed hands regularly and of others that have stayed with one family as landlord for generations, of changes of inn name in bids to stave off closure, of Friendly Societies based on respective pubs, of hostelries that have come and gone (some with barely a mention) and of others that have stayed and still serve customers.

This is a book which provides a great social history of the north-western part of Herefordshire.

This book explores Kilvert's key experiences and relationships and, by placing them securely in the ethos of his period, breaks completely new ground. Its ten chapters provide detailed exploration of his home, his Evangelical upbringing, his Oxford education, the influence of his literary heroes—Wordsworth, Kingsley, Barnes, Tennyson, his work in schools and with the poor, his love for women and children, and his relationship with the gentry. Especially challenging are the new insights into his religious and political beliefs and his relationship with his Clyro vicar.

Close analysis of numerous *Diary* passages illuminates his personality more fully than ever before, as well as the sources of his attitudes and reactions to the social movements of his time. This book offers much to both the Kilvert enthusiast and the reader with a general interest in the Victorian age.

FRANCIS KILVERT was born at Hardenhuish near Chippenham on 3 December 1840, the second child of the parish's rector, Robert Kilvert. The family came originally from Shropshire but towards the end of the 18th century moved to Bath, where Kilvert's grandfather set up a coachbuilding business in Widcombe. The business failed and he became bankrupt. Kilvert's father married Thermuthis Coleman, daughter of Walter Coleman and Thermuthis Ashe. The Ashe family lived at Langley Burrell, Wiltshire, and Robert Kilvert later became rector there. Kilvert attended the school run by his father at Hardenhuish Rectory and that of his uncle at Claverton Down, Bath. After Wadham College, Oxford, he was ordained and acted briefly as curate to his father at Langley Burrell before becoming curate to Richard Lister Venables in Clyro, Radnorshire, in 1865. It was during his seven year stay there that he began keeping his Diary. He returned in 1872 to serve his father again in Langley Burrell before a short spell as Vicar of St. Harmon in Radnorshire. Finally, he became Vicar of Bredwardine, Herefordshire, in November 1877. He married Elizabeth Rowland on 20 September 1879 but died five weeks later of peritonitis.

JOHN TOMAN spent 30 years as a teacher, lecturer and inspector of schools. He first read Kilvert's *Diary* in 1975 and began research on *Kilvert: The Homeless Heart* in 1993. He lives in Bristol.

Also from Logaston Press

The Book of Hay

by Kate Clarke
price £6.95

The aim of the book is to provide the visitor to Hay with a feel for the town and surrounding area by giving a brief outline of the historical events and people (both Welsh and English) that have helped to shape it—de Neufmarché, de Breos, King John, de Bohun, King Henry III, de Montfort, the Llywelyns and many more besides who have passed through, ravaged or stayed.

As times became more settled, so traders and merchants grew in importance, as did the struggles to use the Wye as a trade route (barges were actually built in Hay). Agricultural markets grew, associated businesses came and went, religious changes filtered through.

With the coming of the railways, cheaper competition from further afield caused many businesses to falter, whilst more recently a 'new' trade of second hand books and associated literary festivals has brought new vigour.

Extracts from the diary of Francis Kilvert, written whilst he was a curate at nearby Clyro, add to the atmosphere of Victorian Hay and the account of the famous Major Armstrong murder case brings to life the town in the 1920s. Also featured are some of the people who have, in more recent years, played their part in Hay's survival and development, not least Richard Booth, self-styled King of Hay.

Kate Clarke, crime-writer and diarist, moved from London to Hay in 1982. Published true crime books include *Murder At The Priory: the Mysterious Poisoning of Charles Bravo* (co-Author, Bernard Taylor) 1988, which was short-listed for The Crime Writers' Association Gold Dagger Award; *The Pimlico Murder: The Extraordinary Case of Adelaide Bartlett*, 1990; *Who Killed Simon Dale & Other Murder Mysteries*, 1993. The first volume of Journal (as Kate Paul) was published in 1997, the second volume has yet to be published and she is currently working on the third volume.